If I Was
the Devil...

Glyn Barrett

Sovereign World

Sovereign World Ltd
PO Box 777
Tonbridge
Kent TN11 0ZS
England

All Scripture quotations are taken from the New International Version
© Copyright 1973, 1978, 1984 by International Bible Society.
Published by Hodder & Stoughton.

ISBN 1 85240 403 5

The publishers aim to produce books which will help to extend and
build up the Kingdom of God. We do not necessarily agree with every
view expressed by the author, or with every interpretation of Scripture
expressed. We expect each reader to make his/her judgement in the
light of their own understanding of God's Word and in an attitude of
Christian love and fellowship.

Cover image by Chris Denham, www.creatorart.com
Cover design by CCD, www.ccdgroup.co.uk
Typeset by CRB Associates, Reepham, Norfolk
Printed in the United States of America

Contents

Dedication

To Dad – the greatest man I have ever known!

To all the teenagers and young adults choosing to be a part of God's "Audacious" generation!

Acknowledgements

My Wife Sophia, more amazing than ever and our great children Georgia and Jaedon – Life is great!

To Mum, thanks for your amazing insight, wisdom and for being the greatest mum a mischievous little boy could ever have. Sian, what a great sister and friend, life is better because of you!

Dave and Jen – thanks for sharing your journey with us, you are the greatest Pastors we could hope for.

Hope City Church, an amazing church, with people who continue to inspire and amaze me.

Dave, Hazel and Gill, thanks for "the edit!"

Mark and Stuart your friendship and support in life are worth more to me than you'll ever know.

To Nick and Caroline, Chris and Gosia, Chris and Louise, Mark and Emily, Andy and Karen, Elaine, Naomi, Nate and Nikki – Wow you guys are my heroes.

Youth Alive, a great network of Youth leaders throughout the UK who dare to dream big dreams and step out into the realm of the "impossible". The years ahead will be awesome!

To my best mate Lee. This book would be empty without you. You are my greatest friend!

Jesus You are phenomenal! "Anything for Your honour!"

Foreword

It's always a seriously cool thing when someone you know
and like releases his or her first CD, appears for the first time
on stage or TV, or writes a first book.

As far as I know, Glyn Barrett doesn't act on stage and he
hasn't made a hit CD – though I probably wouldn't be
surprised if he did. One thing I *do* know: he's written a *really*
good book!

I first met Glyn just after he left one of Australia's
warmest cities to live in the not-so-sunny Manchester, UK.
(You'll read about that part of his life – and why he made
the change – in this book.)

Back then, he was just an ordinary kid who had this glint
in his eye, a look that said, "One day, I'm going to do
something great … Just watch me." These days, he's one of
the UK's finest youth pastors and an associate pastor in a
great church. In his spare time, he heads up a growing
national youth ministry.

All that wouldn't be of much interest to you, I know, if it
weren't for one thing: *it's helped him to produce a great book
that can turn your life around!*

Glyn's a funny guy. Whether he's talking about swimming
"butt naked" on the school swim team, or studying how
dogs explode, or doing 180° turns in a speeding car during

a high-speed escape (all true stories!), he'll have your attention all the way.

Yet he also says some really wise stuff – and that's why I like this book so much.

It's easy to read, hard to put down, and it really makes you think. It's not just about style – there's important substance in here too.

Whether you're a bookworm (translation: "nerd") or a serious non-reader, you'll find you can't stop turning the pages.

Glyn writes like he's speaking to *you* and nobody else and he's talking about some stuff that doesn't get talked about enough ...

The Bible says that you have a spiritual enemy. He's called the devil, or Satan. Some people claim that he doesn't exist. (Ironically, it was Alice Cooper who said: "That's what the devil wants people to believe, that he's just a myth.")

Jesus said that your enemy only wants to destroy you, to steal your God-given destiny. Jesus, on the other hand, came so that you can have life, and have it to the max (see John 10:10).

The Bible famously describes the devil as a roaring lion, a ravenous cat who goes around looking for vulnerable people to sink his vicious teeth into (1 Peter 5:8). *This book is about how you can de-fang your enemy, one sharp tooth at a time.*

This book talks about the devil, but it's not really *about* him – it's about *you*!

It's about how you can rise above the junk that life throws at you; how you can take responsibility for your future (even if you've had a screwed up past).

It's about how you can stop settling for being mediocre and start making choices that give you control of things.

It's about all that and much more.

Anyway, I don't need to rave on any more. *Just get into the book!* I promise, you'll want to give it to your friends (after you've read it again yourself!)

Mal Fletcher
Next Wave International & Edges.tv
June 2004

The part you just HAVE to read!

If I was the devil ...

When I was a kid, I was often called the devil! Don't be alarmed ... I'm not!! But sometimes I got into trouble and sometimes I was a bit mischievous.

Surely that's all part of being a kid? Or so I thought. But it seemed like my misadventures weren't looked on so kindly by some adults. Ok, so I blew up a dog! It wasn't my fault! We made a bomb, put it on a deserted piece of land in Australia somewhere and just happened to find my neighbour's dog liked the smell of the burning wick! The bomb exploded and Cindy the poodle was no more!

Sure, I burnt down the beautiful ivy that grew up the side of the neighbour's house! But it wasn't my fault! How was I to know that fire liked dead leaves? Maybe we went a bit far with shooting real hunting arrows in a light-hearted game of bows and arrows? Perhaps shooting air rifles at each other went a bit far? But it was all in fun!

I definitely know it wasn't my fault when I turned the hosepipe on a neighbour who was riding his motorbike down the street, making him crash into a tree. Surely he knew the tree was there? Why didn't he just avoid it?

I'll admit some of my practical jokes went a bit far. Like the time I thought it would be hilarious to play cricket on the church roof during a deacons' meeting, or the incident with my sister's bra on my head during her first date!

But one thing is certain: I wasn't malicious. I just wanted to have fun and sometimes I acted first and thought later!

That's probably why I was called "the devil" by mums, friends, church elders, deacons, fathers and teachers! (One teacher told me, when I asked him to sign my end of year book, that he would only sign my death certificate – Cheers!)

Having been brought up in the church, the son of a minister, and having been involved in youth pastoring for 15 years, I have seen a few things. I have seen youth come and go. I've seen them pray and make great declarations before God and I have seen those same awesome youth walk away from God! The amazing thing is that it always seems to be the same reasons, the same excuses and the same circumstances that cause youth to walk away from destiny, hope, joy, peace and the brilliant time that God offers.

This book is written to youth, young adults and their pastors. Paul says in Galatians 5:7 *"You were running a good race. Who cut in on you ... ?"* The answer? Sometimes it's the devil and sometimes it's not! (Please don't get me wrong. I'm not a weirdo who believes the devil is behind everything. Sometimes we just make dumb choices and have to live with the consequences.) But this book focuses on the part the devil plays in our misdemeanours (yep – I don't know what that word means either).

The Bible says in 1 Peter 5:8 that the devil is like *"... a roaring lion looking for someone to devour."* Now, I don't mind him roaring, freaky though it may be – it's the devouring part that frightens me. And let's face it, he's had thousands of years' experience in leading young people away from God, getting them to the point where he devours them.

It's about time the Daniel generation rose up and shut the mouth of the lion. Daniel was in the lions' den (Daniel chapter 6), where the lions weren't just roaring, they were about to start devouring too! They were hungry! But Daniel's courage, integrity and pursuit of God shut the mouth of the lions.

In your life the devil may be roaring loudly, but if we take out his teeth – what can he do? This book is like a dentist's surgery. One by one we are going to take out the devil's teeth, so that he can no longer make young people believe the lies he has fed them for thousands of years. If he's got no teeth – he'll just have to try and gum us to death!

Read this book and it'll change your life. Put it on the shelf and it'll just get dusty. Go on, I dare you – read it!

You see, if I was the devil, the first thing I would do is
... **help you find an excuse NOT to read it!!**

Have fun – I know you will – but above all, be empowered! You're awesome!!!

Glyn

Coming up ...
A very funny story about sperm!

Someone once said:

"Accept that some days
you are the pigeon and
some days the statue."

. . . Don't believe it!

Tooth #1

If I was the devil I would make you ...

... a victim not a victor

I'll never forget when I first realised that life could be unfair.
I was five years old and my Dad had helped me to build my
first model toy. It was a black van, exactly like the one off
the 1980's TV show, *The A-Team*. It had cool wheels,
blacked out windows and even the red stripe down the side. I
was so proud that I ran out into the lounge room to show
Uncle Rodney. (He wasn't really my uncle, just a good friend
of the family.) I thought, "If anyone will be impressed with
my van, it's Uncle Rodney!"

He picked it up and "oohed" and "aahed" in all the right
places and then, just when I was satisfied that he had given
me an appropriate response, dropped it and broke it. I was
heartbroken. The trouble was my mum wouldn't let me stay
angry. I had to forgive him. I decided from that moment on
that life wasn't fair!

The story of my model van is nothing in comparison with
what some young people go through.

I'll never forget the first time a young girl sat in my office
with my wife and me to tell us that she had been continually
abused by her relatives since the age of nine.

I'll never forget the time a guy at school committed

suicide, or the time a friend's baby died, or the time a friend took an overdose, or the time, or the time, or the time ...

What do you say at times like that? To be honest, it took me ages to know how to deal with situations like that. And the truth is that similar situations are happening every day all over the world. Maybe something like that has happened or is happening to you? A lot of young people simply lie down and take it thinking, "That's just the life I ended up with ..." End of story.

The reason is because,

> ... if I was the devil I would try to make you ...
> ... a victim not a victor

A few years ago, a friend from Sydney came to visit us. We picked him up from the airport and knowing that he was a Greek Aussie coffee-lover, we stopped for a cup of Espresso. Two hours and about 900 coffees later (I'm still not sleeping well because of the caffeine overdose!) we decided to take him to our house.

Everything in our street was as we left it: the dogs from the house on the left (who I wished I could use a bomb on) were barking, as usual, and the neighbours on the right were watching TV, as usual. The neighbours across the road to the right were washing their car in the rain (typical English summer) and the neighbours across the road to the left were watching between the curtains to see what this barmy "vicar" was up to now!

My wife unlocked the door and walked in – noticing nothing. As soon as I walked through the door I realised something was wrong. The clue was simple: the back door was wide open and covered in great big dents where a crowbar had been used to bash it in!

You guessed it – someone had broken into our house. The amazing thing was that nothing had been stolen. In fact, we had arrived home just as the thieves were getting into the house. We know this because our other neighbours (from around the corner and eight houses up on the left), were walking their dogs (no bomb needed) on the path behind our back fence, when the dogs pinned our potential thieves up against a wall!

We contacted the police, filed a report and then two days later received some mail from them. The mail read:

You have been a victim of crime!

I have to admit, it didn't reassure me! I knew I was a victim of crime. I just wanted to make sure it didn't happen again. I bought a burglar alarm, a security light (which I still can't get to work) and new, improved locks. Everything I needed to make sure the thieves didn't get at my house again.

We then bought a shed. Guess what? The thieves loved that as well. Eventually I put my brain into action and came up with a simple theory – MESS! If I can't find anything in the shed, then neither will the thieves! Two years later and no more break-ins! One day however, I decided to clean out the shed. I put in new shelves, cabinets, cupboards and toolboxes. In fact, it was probably the best looking shed you've ever seen. Then the thieves struck again. They left a note saying, "Thanks for cleaning the shed. Now we can find what we want to steal." Well, not really, but they might as well have written something like that! SO, the shed remains a mess ...

During the summer, we put up a gazebo (material type) to have one of the great Aussie BBQs I'd become accustomed to over my years in Australia. Guess what? After two nights that too was gone, even the pegs!

Now, I live in a nice place. I have a nice house, nice friends and nice neighbours (apart from the dogs on the left – who I think have a death wish!) I don't deserve this type of aggro!

Actually, that's the point! Nobody deserves that type of aggravation. I didn't choose to be a victim (Yep, you guessed it. The police sent me that reassuring letter again when the gazebo got nicked.)

You never *ask* to be a victim, it just happens. Things that are out of our control happen to us. They may be of a sexual or physical nature, or of a mental nature – who knows? But stuff happens! (or as the Christian bumper sticker reads – "Poo happens"!)

But there is a big difference between *being* a victim and living with a "victim mentality". A "victim" is someone who has had something happen to them. The "victim mentality" is a learned behaviour pattern which continually affects the way a person thinks, acts and lives because of something that took place.

Let me explain what I mean. I have had my shed broken into three times. Each time, my neighbours (the TV watchers), came to give me their commiserations. My answer each time has been, "Oh well, it's only a shed!" I was a "victim". But when their shed was broken into they said, "This is always happening to us, it's not fair. Why does this happen to us?" They had a victim mentality.

When the victim mentality is translated into everyday life it sounds like this:

- I can't do this because I've never been able to do it before.
- It's just too hard.
- Everybody says that about me.
- It's not fair.
- It always happens to me.
- I can't because (excuse, excuse, excuse ...).

Maybe you find yourself saying things like this. If so, you have a victim mentality. Something happened to you and it's affecting the way you think, act, dream and live.

It becomes a constantly repeating behaviour pattern. You can't seem to stop thinking that way because you're constantly *reinforcing* that way of thinking. And guess who's behind it all? (Yep, you guessed it) – the devil!

Just imagine that you were a serial murderer (not of dogs, but people). You had personally been responsible for the death of many innocent men, women and children. You killed them just because they believed different things from those that you believe. Are you imagining? Well, you are imagining the life of the Apostle Paul. He was responsible for killing many people because he didn't believe the news about Salvation through Jesus. One day, he had an encounter with God (Acts 9) and became a Christian. If this was you, what do you do now? You are a Christian, but guilty of murder! What was the key to Paul's success? In Philippians 3:13 Paul says, *"... But **one** thing I do: forgetting what is behind and straining toward what is ahead ... "*

That's the key that can rip the teeth from the devil. Forget what has happened and move on with your life.

If you have had something (or many things) happen to

you which has made you learn to live with a victim mentality then there are some things you can do so you no longer believe what the devil is continually trying to make you believe.

There are three decisions you need to make to help you extract the first tooth of "victim mentality" and strip the devil of his grin and grip on your life and future: *Choose to believe God has a great life for you*; *Refuse to live in "the circle of no control"* and *Choose God*.

1. Choose to believe God has a great life for you

Do you remember Sports Day at school? The blood, the sweat, the tears, the embarrassment! (Which reminds me, look out for the swimming story – it really happened to me and it nearly destroyed my life, whilst others laughed for years!) Sports Day at school was not the first time you were in a competition.

Once upon a time, you entered a race! Actually, you had no say in whether or not you wanted to run (very similar to Sports Day at school). This particular race began before you were born because this race was between *sperm!* When your biological mother and father got together, sperm was the result and you were one of millions of sperm. The rules of the race were very simple: *the first one to the egg wins!* So imagine race day. The judge is reading out the rules (which doesn't take long, because there is only one) and then the starter's gun goes off and you begin to run, err, swim (after all, you are sperm)! There you are with millions of other potential brothers and sisters, swimming your little heart out, with your tail waggling and your head bobbing. Through this tube and that tube you go, when all of a

sudden you realise you are in the lead! Amazing! In a
moment of absolute madness and boasting, you turn around
and poke out your tongue to all your competitors – which
was a foolish move because millions of them overtake you.
So you turn around and swim your little heart out again.
One hundred thousand by one hundred thousand you
overtake them; through this tube, through that tube when all
of a sudden one little sperm yells out: "THE EGG!!!" at
which point everyone charges towards the egg – but guess
what? YOU GET THERE FIRST! You and the egg get together
and nine months later a beautiful little boy (or girl) is born –
YOU! You started out life as a champion. The first ever race
you were in, you won. You were born a champion!
Somewhere in you right now is that champion dying to get
out!

Whenever you find yourself slipping into the "victim"
way of thinking, remember you were born a champion
because you were designed by God as a champion. Did you
get that? You were designed by God! He knows all about
you because He created you.

In Jeremiah 1:5 it says,

> *"Before I formed you in the womb I knew you,*
> *before you were born I set you apart;*
> *I appointed you ..."*

What an awesome verse!
Who did the forming? God!
Who did the knowing? God!
Who did the setting apart? God!
Who appointed you? God!
When did He do it? Before you were in the womb! In other

words, before the starter said, "First one to the egg wins!" Before that race, God knew you!

The Hebrew word for "knew" or "know" is the word *yada*, and it actually talks about God knowing us in several different ways:

▶ *To have knowledge of someone*

The first thing *yada* means is to have *knowledge* of someone. David Beckham is a famous footballer. I can honestly say that I have never met David, BUT, if you are like me, you know everything about him. You know where he gets his hair cut, where he shops, where he lives, his favourite food, etc. It's not that I care, I don't ask to know, I just know. It's because the newspapers, magazines and TV shows are full of this famous player. I don't know him personally, but I can honestly say that I have knowledge of him! I also have knowledge of the Queen, the Prime Minister, even Denzel Washington!

So when God said He "knew" you before you were born, He was saying that He had knowledge of you in the same way you can have knowledge of a famous person.

▶ *Acquaintance*

But it doesn't stop there. *Yada* also means that God was an *acquaintance* of ours. It's like me walking through a shopping mall whilst Becks is coming the other way. When he sees me he calls out, "Hey Glyn, how ya doing? The weather's great! I am joining Manchester City Football Club because I have eventually seen the light!" And we continue to chat about stuff that is not too deep and meaningful. He is my acquaintance. We are simply friends.

So when God says He "knew" us, it meant that He was an acquaintance of ours.

▶ *Intimate acquaintance*

But it doesn't stop there. *Yada* also means to be an *intimate acquaintance* of someone. So now we are not just talking about football, the weather and other non-important stuff, we are talking about stuff that really matters – dreams, ambitions, hopes etc. He was so intimate with us that He thought through and planned what an amazing life we could have if we simply made the choice to live for Him.

Listen to some verses in the Bible which tell us more about how intimate God is with us:

- *"You knit me together in my mother's womb"* (Psalm 139:13). God put you together!
- *"All the days ordained for me were written in your book before one of them come to be"* (Psalm 139:16). God has a purpose for each and every day you live!
- *"Search me O God, and know my heart; test me and know my anxious thoughts ... "* (Psalm 139:23). He is so intimate – He knows what you think!
- *" ... the very hairs of your head are all numbered ... "* (Luke 12:7). God is so close to you – He can count your hairs!!!
- *" ... He* [God] *knows the secrets of the heart ... "* (Psalm 44:21). God knows what your closest friend doesn't!

And that's just a few!

Wow, BEFORE you were born the Bible says that God knew you! It means that He had knowledge of you, was an acquaintance of yours, and was intimately involved with you – even BEFORE the race began.

Someone who lives with a victim mentality is prone to be

an excellent excuse maker. The victim reads verses in the Bible like Jeremiah 29:11 which says, *" 'For I know the plans I have for you,' declares the LORD, 'Plans to prosper you and not to harm you, plans to give you a hope and a future' "*, and makes excuses as to why "their" particular future is not included in this verse.

When God says, "I want you to be awesome and do incredible things!" we do what Moses did in Exodus 3 and 4 (Moses had a victim mentality too). We begin to list the reasons why we can't change our lives and be awesome for God (see Exodus 3:1–4:17):

- **Who am I?** (3:11) – In other words, I am a nobody! I can't really do something that counts because I am simply me! If I was like someone else (and we list friends, famous people etc.) ...
- **What happens if it doesn't work?** (paraphrase of 3:13) – In other words, my fear of failure is greater than my desire to change or see transformation. So I'll do nothing, just in case the something that I do makes things even worse!
- **I'm not talented or gifted enough!** (4:10) – In other words, I don't have the talents and abilities to be anything other than what I am and have now. This is me – take me or leave me, I can't change!
- **Must be a case of mistaken identity!** (4:13) – In other words, I can't do it. Someone else needs to take responsibility for me. I'm the victim here!

The excuses we give God for not rising up to achieve His destiny for our lives are not enough to throw God off His passion to see us be the champions we were born to be. If you are a Christian, then the Bible says that God lives within you. God knew you from before the world began. You are a spiritual being, but the victim mentality is a series of excuses based on earthly experiences. And although they hurt and many of those incidents are truly tragic (and God's heart hurts for you), He says to you, "C'mon, I know you; I set you apart; I appointed you – you are spiritual – you are awesome!"

2. Refuse to live in the "Circle of no control"

One of the best books I have read on understanding youth is *The Seven Habits of Highly Effective Teens* by Sean Covey.[1] In that book he talks about "the circle of no control".

In our lives there are things that we *do* control and things that we *don't* control. Things that we don't control include the things we have no choice over:

- The weather: sun, rain, hail, wind etc.
- Family background: mum, dad, brothers and sisters.
- Money.
- Other people: responses, choices, attitudes.
- Isolated incidents: abuse, tragedy, accidents.
- Traffic jams, shopping queues.
- McDonald's Ice cream machine not working (again!).

These belong in the circle of no control. We did not choose for them to happen. The amazing thing is, we can spend a lot of time arguing and complaining about the things that happen in this circle. Even though we did not determine them, we spend a lot of time living there! The result of this is

[1] Sean Covey, *The Seven Habits of Highly Effective Teens*, Fireside, 1998.

that we end up saying, "The weather ruined my day," or "McDonalds ruined my day," or "That person ruined my day," or even worse, "That incident/abuse ruined my life."

The trouble with this is that we are effectively giving away the power of our life to some other person, action, or even a machine! If your afternoon has been ruined because McDonalds ran out of ice cream, then you have given the power of your life over to Ronald McDonald. You are effectively saying that McDonalds has power over you!

Sounds silly doesn't it? Well, that's because it is! If I was the devil, that's what I'd do – tie you into the circle of no control!

You may have had some terrible things happen to you at some time in your life. It would be a shame to let that have power over you for the rest of your life. You only have one life. Don't give it away!

When I began full time as a minister in a church, I was 24 years old and to be honest, I had no idea what to do with all the hours in my week (Don't tell the boss!). I thought I would fill them in by reading 1 and 2 Timothy in the Bible. The Apostle Paul wrote both of those books to a young pastor called ... you guessed it ... Timothy, giving instruction on what to do as a young minister. I read 1 and 2 Timothy every week for one year (at least that killed a bit of time!). 1 Timothy 4:12 says, *"Don't let anyone look down on you because you are young, but set an example for the believers in speech, in love, in faith and in purity."* I preached to youth at meetings, conferences and events from this verse about being an example, not being intimidated and the ingredients of faith and purity etc. Even with all that preaching, I missed the power of the verse! The first two words say: *"Don't let"*!

In other words, Paul was saying; "Timothy, if you feel intimidated, that's because you have allowed yourself to be intimidated. You let it happen! You gave the power of your life away. You gave your permission to be intimidated!" Paul is encouraging Timothy to take back his permission and not let others intimidate him any more.

You could draw a circle and write in it everything that has happened to you that you had no control over – the weather, your family, even abuse. Make a decision from today to refuse to live in the circle of no control any longer. Don't give your permission for those things to have power over you any more. Choose to live instead in the "circle of control". The circle of control includes:

- Your decisions
- Your actions
- Your attitudes and mindsets.

Ask God to help you today to not let things overwhelm you any longer and to rise up with right decisions and a brand new attitude to match!

I recently heard a tragic story about a young woman who was walking in a park one night, when a man attacked her and violently beat her, leaving her to die in some bushes. She crawled out of the bushes and made her way to the street and flagged down the nearest car. When the car stopped, she was horrified to discover that the man driving the car was the same man who had just beaten her. He again attacked and beat her leaving her to die. When the police finally arrived on the scene, they were horrified to find this lady close to death. They quickly admitted her to hospital and were amazed that as she recovered from her ordeal, she had no bitterness or resentment in her heart. When they asked her why she was not in distress over the incident, she replied, "That man took one night of my life, but he's not going to take the rest of my life!"

What an amazing woman! Her attitude was that she was going to live in the circle of control, NOT the circle of no control! She couldn't control the fact that that man attacked her – that is a "no control" area. But she could control how she was going to respond to it and what her attitude would be like later. Instead of letting that incident ruin her future, she made the decision – "it will not". What was she doing? She was not giving her permission for that one night to ruin her life.

3. Choose God!

The last thing you can do to get out of the victim mentality is not to date someone who looks like a barn door, is a gossip, a nag and sometimes looks like she has two bearded men in a headlock! (Obviously a guy's perspective – but you get the gist!)

My best mate is called Lee. Lee and I grew up together in Australia – same street, same school, same youth group, same church, same Bible College, same girlfriends (kidding!).

At one particular time in our friendship, I remember Lee running into my room with a grin on his face and a look of love in his eyes. When I asked him what was going on, he replied, "I'm in love!" Now Lee wasn't one for falling in and out of love, so this was big news! When I asked him who the poor unfortunate soul was, he replied, "Who else but Fiona!" (Not really her name, but for the sake of anonymity and my desire not to get sued, we'll keep her real name a secret!)

When he shared her name with me, I nearly fell off the chair! "Fiona, you've got to be joking!" I *felt* like saying, "She looks a little like a barn door, is a gossip, a nag, and to make matters worse, she sometimes looks like she has two bearded men in a headlock!" (Forgive me, but I was young and prone to unpleasant thoughts at times! I know my thinking was wrong and cruel! I'm sorry!) That's what I was thinking, *but I said*, "Fiona? That's fantastic! She's a lovely girl. I think you should take time to get to know her a little bit more – in a group maybe – before you start going out with her!"

Lee replied, "Good idea!" at which point he walked off singing, "The weather outside is frightful, but the fire is so delightful ... " which really didn't make any sense because it was Australia and 34 degrees Celsius in the shade! Yep, he had certainly gone mad!

A few weeks later, Lee ran into my room, threw a book at my head and proceeded to pin me up against a wall whilst throwing punches into my stomach! When he calmed down I said, "What are you doing, Poo?" (That was his nickname and that has a funny story too.) He said, "I can't believe it!" "What?" I replied. To which he shouted, "Fiona! She ...

- ... looks a little like a barn door! (I said, "I know!")
- ... is a gossip (I said, "I know!")
- ... is a nag (I said, "I know!")
- ... and to make matters worse, sometimes she looks like she has two bearded men in a headlock!" (I said, "I know!")

To which he shouted, "So, why didn't you tell me all that when I first asked you?" I answered, "I thought it would just be a good laugh!"

Can you believe that? So much for friendship! I was in it for the laugh and this was my mate's life we were dealing with.

That pretty much reminds me of the devil. He doesn't care about you at all. In fact, he hates you more than you can ever imagine. His sole desire is to destroy your soul and leave it desolate. He screams at you, "Do whatever the hell you want to do, because that's where I want to take you!" He says, "There are no rules, no rights and no wrongs – do anything you want." And the truth is even scarier than this ... usually we do.

We live life at times like a madman behind the wheel of a car (see later). We do whatever we want, we don't care in the same way I didn't care if Lee and Fiona got hurt. The devil pushes you on, urges you to do more and more with your life without regard for your future.

On one side the devil says, "Do whatever you want. I don't care because I hate you and want to destroy you!" On the other side we have God. He says things like,

- "For I know the plans I have for you ... plans to prosper you and not to harm you, plans to give you hope and a future" (Jeremiah 29:11).
- "I *want you* to have life and have it to the full" (John 10:10).
- "If you believe in me you will live ... " (John 11:25).
- " ... in all things I work for the *good* of those who love me, who have been called according to *my purpose*" (Romans 8:28).
- " ... *you* are more than *a conqueror* ... " (Romans 8:37).
- " ... neither death nor life, neither angels nor demons, neither the present nor the future, nor any powers,

neither height nor depth, nor anything else in creation, will be able to separate *you* from *my love ...* " (Romans 8:38–39).

Given the choice, I think I'd choose God every time. You would have to be a nutter to want to live for the devil.

In Psalm 18:16–19, it says, *"He* [God] *reached down from on high and took hold of me; he drew me out of deep waters. He rescued me from my powerful enemy ... the LORD was my support."* Verse 35 continues to say, *"... you* [God] *stooped down to make me great."*

WOW! God reaches down to you! He stretches out His hand to you to pick you up because He wants to make you great! How awesome is that?

How does God make you great?

- He plants you in a great church! (Psalm 1).
- He speaks to you through the Bible (Psalm 119:105).
- He gives you peace when you need it (John 14:27).
- He gives you wisdom when you ask for it (James 1:5).
- He gives you power when you need it (Acts 1:8).
- You read this book!

He rescued you to make you great! Make the choice to live for God and blank the devil. He doesn't care about you, so why not reciprocate and not care about him! You can get out of the victim mentality because God is committed to your greatness. Choose God!

29

Pulling out tooth #1

When you live with a victim mentality, it can feel like every day the devil is choosing your wardrobe and that your t-shirt says,

You have been a victim of crime!

Now maybe that's true. Stuff has happened. But just tell the devil, "I won the race!" He'll know what you mean!

If the devil sends you a note saying, "You have been a victim of crime", tell him, "Maybe! But I am not giving the power of my life away to something that happened in my past or is happening right now. I am not giving my permission for that to affect me any longer. I am going to live in the circle of control! And then tell him the sperm story again – just for the heck of it!

If the devil has been making sure you live with a victim mentality, you feel pretty much like the writer of Psalm 18 – in deep waters. The great news is that God has stretched His hand out to you and if you take Him by the hand, He'll make you great! Sure, you have a powerful enemy (the devil), *BUT* God is even more powerful and you *WITH* God make a majority!

So how do you take God's hand to get out of the deep waters? Remember:

1. Choose to believe God has a great life for you.
2. Refuse to live in the circle of no control!
3. Choose God!

A few years ago in America (have you noticed how everything happens in America?), a woman travelled for several hours to see her favourite baseball team play. After a few innings, it became clear that her team was not only going to lose, but they were going to be thrashed! Halfway through the game, she stood in utter disgust and screamed, "I didn't come all this way to see you lose!" The fans laughed and joked, but the players heard the lady and played with renewed attitude and determination. Can you guess what happened? The players turned the game around and her team won.

You know, Jesus says the same thing to you today. He says, "I didn't die on the cross to watch you lose. You are a champion. You can fight and break the mentality of a victim and think about yourself in the way I think about you."

If I was the devil I would try to make you a victim and not a victor. If I was you, I would tell the devil to push off because you have chosen to live the life God died for you to live!

Coming up...

The art of swimming naked!!

Making it real for you!

1. Life can teach you to feel anything but the champion you were destined to be. What excuses have you been using as a reason not to rise up and be God's champion?

. . . .
. . . .
. . . .
. . . .

2. Write in the "circle of no control" everything in your life that you have no control over and choose not to dwell on them or complain about them ever again.

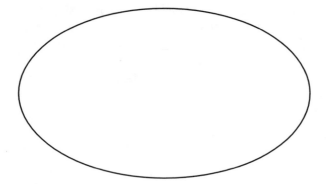

3. Which three areas in your life do you actively need to choose God in? i.e. *choosing God when my friends pressure me . . .*

   (a) . . . .
   (b) . . . .
   (c) . . . .

Someone once said ...

"The other day I was in bed,
looking up at the stars
and thought to myself
'Where the heck is the ceiling?'"

Tooth #2

If I was the devil I would make you think ...

... it's too late!

Oh, how I wish I could live 1985 all over again. It was a tough year all round and quite frankly, if I had the chance to do it again, I would do some things differently.

In 1985 I was living in Toowoomba, Australia. At the time it was a city of 80,000 people. The Garden City of Australia, it was well known for being beautiful (lots of flowers), middle class and very sports orientated. In 1985 I started High School. I was 13 years old and keen to impress. Do you remember what it's like starting for the first time in High School?

Teenagers are like dogs! Not that they eat like them or smell like them, or look like them for that matter, but dogs like to mark out their territory. They do it by urinating at different points in order to say, "Hey dog, this is my territory. When you smell my wee, you better watch out because you are on my turf!" Now, teenagers at school are very similar. They don't wee in random places (although the stairwell in C block always had a strange smell), but 1st year in high school is very important. It's the year that each student is labelled as either cool or a geek; popular or a freak! You mark out your territory by the clubs you join, the subjects you take, the sports teams you join, the acts of

heroism you perform *OR* the embarrassing things you do!
Unfortunately for me, it was the latter that marked me out!

My school was sports mad. We were divided into four
different "houses" for sporting purposes and then we
represented our house in swimming galas, sports days etc. I
was in "Thomson House", famous for its great sportsmen
and women. In fact some from that house have gone on to
represent Australia in various sports. My attempt at
becoming a champion swimmer failed at the first attempt.

I was 13, trying to mark out my territory as *COOL* and the
swimming gala came along. Our house had already won a
few races when it came time for me to represent the house in
"Grade 8, 50 metre freestyle!" How hard could it be? All I
had to do was swim 50 metres (I had been doing it since I
was 5). A doddle, no worries, no problem!

So, picture the scene with me. There I am, standing on the
blocks ready to go. To my left is a grandstand seating
hundreds of people. Thompson House is cheering and
waving its green and gold colours. My heart is pounding
with fear, nerves and excitement and this was *my moment* to
mark out my territory (no, I didn't wee in the pool!).

The starter said, "To your blocks, ready" and *bang*, the
gun went off.

I remember diving into the pool thinking, "Here's my
chance!" I also remember feeling light, free and streamlined
as I began to swim with everything that was within me.
Before long I became conscious of the fact that I was in third
place. The crowd also, was louder than usual! They were not
just cheering, but also laughing hysterically and I felt
encouraged to go on to my destiny and win the race (well, at
least get in the top three!). As I swam, I kept glancing up at
the grandstand, wondering what all the commotion and

laughing was about. I thought to myself, "Self, it goes well, you are in a top three position, you are marking out your territory well. Yep, it all goes well!" We stretched to touch the wall and I discovered I got third! Meanwhile the crowd was still cheering and laughing. As I swam under the lane ropes to get to the steps and out of the pool, one of the referees leaned across the edge of the pool and said, "Good race, Glyn, you swam well!" With great pride I said, "Thanks!" at which point he replied – you guessed it – "Now you had better go back and get your shorts!" Sure enough, when I dived into the pool, my shorts fell off and I swam the whole race *BUTT NAKED* ! And if that wasn't bad enough, they made me swim back to get my shorts!

All did not go well in 1985 and it was yet to get worse! I wish God would let me go back in time to replace or erase that year! Unbelievable!

Yet, the truth is simple: despite the fact that I still find it hard to come to terms with, it's too late! It's happened and I can't go back in time and do it again! Time has gone on that one.

As Christians, stuff happens. We have good days where we feel like we can take on the world for God. But then we also have days where we feel like we've just swum butt naked in front of hundreds of people.

As a Youth Pastor, I have seen young people stand and make the most fantastic decision they could ever make – to follow God and do anything He asks them to do. But then something happens. Somewhere along the line, that incredible young person, with an awesome future in God, makes *a mistake.* Maybe you are that young person and you are saying right now, "Hey, I have made a mistake, in fact, loads of them!"

Maybe you got involved with the wrong crowd. Maybe you've been doing stuff or watching stuff you shouldn't have. Maybe you said something, maybe ... there are hundreds of maybes!

If I was the devil, I would be whispering in your ear ...

"... it's too late!"

I would be reminding you of the times you prayed those awesome prayers, telling you the mistakes you have made and whispering, "There's no going back – you've blown it – it's too late for you to be awesome for God!"

Did you know that the world is full of people who used to be Christians, but made a mistake and believed the lie that said, "It's too late!" How do you answer this accusation? It's easy, really. Start with remembering what the Gospel is all about. Let me explain ...

Remember – what is the Gospel all about?

The word "Gospel" means "good news". If that is true, then why is it that sometimes you meet Christians who look like they have just stepped on an upturned power plug on the floor? (Have you ever done that? *PAIN* is the only word that comes to mind. In fact, I am convinced that the inventors of the three-pronged power plug created it just to cause us pain. I say: "Ban the plug!")

Some Christians look like they are continually walking around with that upturned power plug stuck to their feet. They frown, they sigh, they complain a little (or a lot). You could sometimes think that "Gospel" means: "upturned three-pronged power plug stuck to your feet, causing much pain and misery"! But honestly, "Gospel" means "good news".

In the beginning, God created the perfect world. In Genesis 1:31, God called the world "good". When God calls something good, you have to understand that it is not like my daughter calling her chocolate ice-cream good. When God says it was "good", it meant perfect! But in this perfect world, there was a crafty little serpent. The serpent used to be God's Worship Leader (Lucifer), but he himself wanted to be God, and so God cast him out of heaven. When the devil saw God's perfect creation and Adam and Eve, he was determined to destroy the perfection, so he set out to distract Adam. He did it firstly by making Eve feel like a victim (see Tooth #1). In Genesis 3:1 we read,

> *"Now the serpent was more crafty than any of the wild animals the LORD God had made. He said to the woman, 'Did God really say, "You must not eat fruit from any tree in the garden?"'"*

In Verse 5 he continues,

> *"For God knows that when you eat of it your eyes will be opened, and you will be like God, knowing good and evil!"*

The devil made Eve think, "It's not fair, I'm a victim here. God hasn't told us the full truth. We can have more and God hasn't told us about it!" In other words, they now had an "excuse" to sin. Their excuse was their desire to "have more". This tempting by the devil led Eve and then Adam to eat the fruit. Their act of disobedience brought sin into the world. Romans 5:12 tells us that *"... sin entered the world through one man ... "* The one man who sinned was Adam!

At that point, everything changed. The relationship between God and man broke down. Sickness started, pain started, and a little while later, crime started when Adam's son, Cain, killed his brother Abel.

Imagine how God must have felt at this point. I was heartbroken when Uncle Rodney broke my A-Team truck, but God must have been more so when Adam brought sin into the world. This perfect world, with no pain, no hurt, no death, no sickness, no divorce, no abuse, no crying, was changed in a moment. All because one man believed the lie that he was a victim!

Imagine how the devil was feeling at this point – elated, happy, over the moon. The devil doesn't want you to have what God has planned for your life. He wants your life to be full of the stuff that entered the world when Adam sinned. The pain, hurt, death, sickness, divorce, abuse, crying, loneliness is all that the devil wants for your life. He has designed it that way!

I am sure that the devil would have been saying, "Ha! I got you Adam. The perfect world, you ruined it, wrecked it, destroyed it. There's no going back. It's too late! You'll never walk with God any more! (Genesis 3:8). You'll never have a friendship with God ever again. And as for living forever, you're gonna die Adam – Ha Ha Ha Ha – it's too late now!" And at that point I can hear God say, *"OH REALLY?"*

You see, in Genesis 3:14–15 God talks to the devil and says, "Oi, Loser! [my translation], I'm going to destroy you, because my Son is going to leave heaven and come to earth and fix what you broke! Eat dirt!"

And literally, that's what happened when Jesus came to earth. Listen to what Colossians says about what Jesus did when He died on the cross:

> *"When you were dead in your sins ... God made you alive with Christ. He forgave us **all** our sins ... He took it away, nailing it to the cross ... [It's about to get better – tell the devil this one – he hates it] ... and having disarmed the powers and authorities, he made a public spectacle of them ... [in other words, as my friends in East London would say, 'He was 'avin a larf!' in their faces] ... triumphing over them by the cross."*
>
> (Colossians 2:13–15)

What does that mean? It means "It's not too late!" Can we have a relationship with God? *YES*. Can He forgive us? *YES*. Can we live for God again? *ABSOLUTELY!* Will the devil tell you it's too late? *PROBABLY!* Is it? *NO!* Can we stand before God again and pray that awesome prayer, "Here I am God. I am prepared to do anything for you!"? *TOTALLY!* In fact, right now, where you are, if you have felt like it's too late, you can pray and say,

> "God, I realise it's not too late. I thought it was. I believed the lie, but thank You that despite the fact that I make mistakes again and again, You always have a plan to turn it around. I'll do my best to live for You, but when I make mistakes, thank You that You forgive me and help me move on. Help me to really receive and take on board Your forgiveness. Amen."

What a great prayer! So then, what does the Gospel mean? It means good news! Why? Because God always fixes what is broken!

Here are two practical ways you can live with the mindset, "It's not too late!"

1. Make the decision to start again

Hey, you thought the swimming naked bit was bad. Well, 1985 got worse! Primary school had been really good. I had a lot of friends and I loved playing "army men"! We would run around at lunchtime shooting each other. Then we would get bored with that and play rugby. I loved rugby! So when I went to High School in 1985, I naively thought that things would be just the same. How wrong was I? Not only did High Schoolers not play "army men", but they also did not like pastors' kids!

At the same time that I went to High School, my dad, who was the Pastor of one of the churches in the city, was responsible for buying 14 acres of land and building a church complex that seated 1,000 people. It was an "architectural wonder"! (No, I don't know what that means either, but I heard an adult say it when I was 13!)

My first year at high school coincided with the opening of our new church building. It didn't take too long for the students in the school to work out that the Pastor who was responsible for this new amazing building had a son, and that son goes to *this* school. If swimming naked wasn't bad enough, my school started to play the game a friend of mine calls "Crucify the Christian". Guess what? I was the Christian!

I used to have the books knocked out of my hands in the corridors, my bike was continually vandalised and I was even hung by my feet from the second floor balcony in Block A!

O yeah, "Crucify the Christian" may have been fun for those watching, but when you're the one being crucified ...

I had arrived at High School with high hopes of having a great time, but things weren't developing as I thought they would. When I started at high school I was confident, outgoing and determined. After three years of ridicule and embarrassment, my shoulders drooped and I began to think of myself as a victim and began to live with a "victim mentality". At church, at home and in my youth group, everything was OK, but at school all was not! I had the confidence battered out of me!

When I turned 15, my dad said to us one night at the dinner table, "I think it would be good for us to go to Manchester in England. There is a church there that has invited us to go and I believe it is the right thing to do." It was a bit of a shock and my sister and I went for a walk in the rain to talk about it. At first I was upset, thinking, "I don't want to leave Australia, the weather is great, the beaches are brilliant, the BBQs are fantastic and I have lots of friends." At that point I remembered, "Hey, I don't have lots of friends!" Even some of my church mates had joined in the fun aimed at me in school. I began to think, "What have I got to lose?"

Some months later, our family flew out of Brisbane, headed for Manchester. It turned out that Manchester Airport was closed and so they redirected our flight to Liverpool. Have you ever been to Liverpool? I grew up in Toowoomba, Australia. It was a beautiful city. The Garden City of Australia. My neighbour (the one I made crash into the tree and burnt his hedge) grew championship orchids! I was used to beauty! I discovered that Liverpool was a little bit different! Beautiful to Liverpudlians I'm sure, but I didn't know what planet I had landed on.

As we got out of the plane and walked across the tarmac to the bus that would take us to Manchester, I suddenly realised that no one in this country knew me. The victim mentality that I had adopted, being the butt of everyone's jokes, was unknown in England. As I walked to the bus, I made a decision. I would throw out everything about me that I didn't like and concentrate on my strengths. I wouldn't live under the shadow of "the person I had become" any more and behave the way people had pigeon-holed me to act. I would be and act the way I wanted to be and act. "This is my life, so I will live it!" (God had a huge part to play in this process. The next point will show His role in it.) On that airport tarmac that day, I had to make the decision, "I choose to change!"

Something happened at that moment. My walk changed, my attitude changed, my confidence returned, because I was finally deciding to be me. When we got off the bus in Manchester, I was the one who approached the people waiting for us. I introduced myself to them, instead of hiding behind my dad. I said how great it was to be in Manchester.

Within weeks of me making this decision, I was the school prefect, I was preaching in the youth meetings, I was in the church band and I had the ability to make lots of friends without repelling them with my victim vibe!

I simply made the decision, *"I CAN START AGAIN!"*

Unfortunately I had to move countries to learn this lesson. However, it wasn't the "moving countries" that ultimately changed me, it was "moving my mindset" – understanding that, "If I choose, I *CAN* start again!" Right where you are, you can make the decision to start again. Listen to what 2 Corinthians 5:17 says:

> *"... if anyone is in Christ [a Christian] he is a new creation; the old has gone, the new has come!"*

God gives you the right and the power to start again. You can wake up in the morning and begin to live with a sense of "newness" about you. He gives you the ability to make that decision. You can say to yourself, "This is my life. I can be who I want to be without being put in a box by my friends!"

Maybe you think, "But it's too far gone. I have been acting this way for years. This is who people know me to be. It's too late. I have made so many mistakes! You really don't understand, Glyn, I have made major boo boos!"

Well, maybe you have. Maybe you have been living the way you have been living for quite a while. Maybe you have made some major mistakes. The only thing I can think to say to you at this point is, "What about Paul in the Bible?" He was a serial murderer of Christians. He was responsible for putting to death many Christian families. If God could change him (Acts 9), then God can change you. God is the expert at taking people's lives and helping them to start again. He has been doing it for thousands of years. He is not surprised by you! He is not scratching His head, saying, "Wow, I've never dealt with anything like this before!" He is saying, "Hey, I can help you to start again. I can make it all new! It's not too late. It's the end of a chapter and time to start a new, fresh chapter in your life!"

2. Remember the first time

I Love soccer. I support Manchester City Football Club. Sometimes they win; sometimes they lose. Sometimes I'm glad I support them and sometimes I wish I did something else – like flower pressing or knitting!

Match day is exciting! Driving to the game, I am full of hope that we will win. People arrive with scarves and banners, singing, shouting and laughing all the way. Everyone is full of anticipation, expecting a great game of football. I remember on one occasion going to a game with a friend. We arrived early to take in some of the atmosphere. We stood with 40,000 people singing the City song, "Blue moon". We cheered as the commentator read out the names of the City players. We booed when he read out the name of the referee and we went ballistic when the City players ran out onto the pitch, then watched in horror as City went three goals down in the first 30 minutes. It was amazing to feel the atmosphere change! The opposition fans were singing, "Who are ya, who are ya?" and the City fans started to go home. There was still an hour left to go, but people were leaving, sad and disheartened. The hope and anticipation that was there 30 minutes earlier had gone.

What would happen if you could roll the clock back 30 minutes and start again? The singing would be back, the hope would be there, the atmosphere would be electric! It's just a pity that at football, you can't start the game again!

Maybe you feel 3–0 down! Maybe you have lost that expectation and anticipation that you once had as a Christian. Well, guess what? *With God's help, starting again is not just something you desire, it can be a reality!*

In Jeremiah 7:12, God in effect says, "Go to the place where I first made a name for myself in your life."

That's the answer! Remember in your life, the time when you first had an encounter with God? Maybe it was in church, or at youth group, or at a youth camp. Remember what He did, what He said and how it changed your life! And as you sit and remember and think about it, you'll find the score going back to 0–0, and you will have a sense that you can start again.

When I was twelve, God did something amazing in my life and I had a real sense that He was with me and had an amazing plan for me. Even now when I feel 3–0 down, I go back in my mind to those times when God first began to stamp His presence and power in my life. I even begin to sing some of the worship songs I used to sing back then as I remember the time when God "first made a name for Himself in my life". As I do that, the focus comes off me. I stop thinking about me and my problems and I am directed more onto Him. In the place of worship, I begin to encounter God again in a fresh way. My heart and spirit become open to Him and I begin to hear Him speaking again into my life through the Bible, preaching, and even His quiet whisper.

You can only start again with God's help! You need to hear Him speak to you, to give you guidance, correction and discipline in order to change. Something amazing happens as you "remember" the time God first made a name for Himself in your life. You find that you want to change, that you want to do things His way, that you were born to be a champion! Somewhere in that process God gives you the power and ability to change the way you think, feel, and ultimately the way you behave.

As I walked across the tarmac in Liverpool that day, I decided to change, but I needed God's help to do it. I later began to put myself in the place of worship, as I had when I was twelve, and God did speak. He did give me direction and guidance. He did reassure me. He did affirm that I could change. And as I listened to and put into practice the Word of God – change came!

Pulling out tooth #2

So what do you think? Is it time to start again? Many of you reading this right now have heard yourself say, "It's too late!" The good news is – it's not! With God there is always a way back, always a way to start afresh, always a way to live and be renewed again and again. It's called – the Gospel! How do you start again?

1. Make the decision to start again.
2. Remember the first time.

Learning to drive is great fun. Understanding the complexities of mirror, signal, manoeuvre, whilst controlling the clutch, accelerating and steering, make the task too difficult for some during their driving test, which is why many fail at their first attempt. I, on the other hand, can boast in the fact that I passed first time! Some of you are yet to learn how to drive. Others of you are doing what *you call* driving (others call scary), and others of you drive well.

Imagine for a moment the nerves and excitement of "driving test day"! You sit in the car, confident that you will pass. You are excited, because in 40 minutes time, you *KNOW* you will be able to drive the car away, unaided, because you have passed your test.

The test begins and at the first intersection you stall the engine. Not a problem – you restart the car and move off. Things are going well until you mount the curb; complete your 3-point turn in $7\frac{1}{2}$ points and bump into (or "rub" as my friend calls it) another car. As you manoeuvre your way back into the test centre the examiner sighs, wipes the sweat from his brow, thanks God for getting him home safely and then turns to you and says, "You have failed your test."

Imagine in that moment your disappointment, frustration, anguish, embarrassment – and then to your amazement he says – "Would you like to start again?" Imagine if they could say that! Imagine if you could re-sit your test straight away. Wouldn't that be awesome?

Great news. God says to you right now, "Would you like to start again?" If the answer is "yes", then why not repeat the prayer we prayed earlier:

> "God, now I realise it's not too late. I thought it was, I believed the lie, but thank You that despite the fact that I make mistakes, again and again, You always have a plan to turn it around. I'll do my best to live for You, but when I make mistakes, thank You that You forgive me and help me move on. Help me to really receive and take on board Your forgiveness. Amen."

Go for it. New life, new creation and new day. You can ...

... START AGAIN!!!

Coming up ...

The really weird Bible!!

Making it real for you!

1. In what three areas of your life do you realise that you need to start again?

   (a) ....

   (b) ....

   (c) ....

2. Write down the time that God first made a name for Himself in your life (i.e. a camp, youth meeting etc.).

   ....

   ....

   ....

3. Make a conscious effort to spend some time worshipping God over those three areas that you want to start again in.

4. Write down a prayer you can pray everyday, asking God to help you change as you worship Him.

   ....

   ....

   ....

   ....

Tooth #3

If I was the devil I would make you think ...

... that'll do

Do you remember getting school projects? Most of the time they were pretty boring. At other times they were downright uncool!

Take the time in Primary School when I was asked to do some knitting for my project! *Me? Knitting?* You must be joking! I was into football, cricket, rugby, playing "army men" and blowing up dogs. Knitting was strictly for girls. I also remember once doing a cross-stitch for a school project – how embarrassing!

There were, however, other times when I actually did projects I enjoyed, like building a model of the solar system or making a chair in woodwork class.

Sometimes I would start a project with loads of enthusiasm, then after realising it wasn't going to be as quick as I had originally thought, I would start to take short-cuts and end up making the famous old statement, *"That'll do!"*

Mal Fletcher writes in his book *Get Real:*[2]

> 'Have you ever seen a dog climbing Mount Everest for the kicks? How about a fun-crazy cat parachuting from a plane at twenty thousand feet? Or a horse bungee

[2] Mal Fletcher, *Get Real*, Nelson Word Ltd, 1993.

jumping? How about a very fit chicken running for Olympic glory? No? Few people have and there's very good reason for this: only human beings are built for heroism. Oh sure, Lassie is one notable exception, but by and large we Homo sapiens have cornered the market on adventurism. Every one of us wants to achieve something memorable and significant.

It's true, only humans have the inbuilt ability to be heroes. But heroism doesn't come cheap or easy. To be a hero, you have to put everything into what you do to be the best you can be.

Here are some ways you can beat the "that'll do" syndrome in your life:

1. Be the hero!

I remember hearing about a true story that took place in New Zealand a few years ago. A mother had picked up her 12-year-old daughter from school in the car and on the way home there was a terrible accident. The car they were travelling in crashed into a petrol tanker. The mother and the truck driver managed to get out, but the daughter (we'll call her Sonia), was trapped in the passenger seat of the car.

The truck driver and the mother tried desperately to rescue the little girl, but they were unable to. Almost immediately, the petrol tanker caught fire and flames licked around the car with Sonia inside. Both her mum and the truck driver stood by helplessly as the fire got hotter and hotter. By this time, the firemen who had arrived on the scene were working hard to put the fire out. They concentrated all the foam onto the burning car in an attempt to save Sonia's life.

As the flames threatened to engulf the car altogether, one of the brave firemen did something that he wasn't trained to do! He dropped his part of the hose and ran into the flames. He made his way to Sonia and tried to free her. She remained trapped in the car. Instead of leaving her there to die, he sat next to her with his arms around her, hugging her to his chest.

For one hour all the firemen concentrated their hoses on that little burning car, with the fireman and Sonia inside. Both the fireman and Sonia nearly died from one of two extremes – the heat was so bad they were nearly burnt to death, and they nearly suffocated because the foam was sucking the oxygen out of the air. (Fire needs oxygen in order to burn. If you can take the oxygen out of the air, the fire dies out!)

For some time, the fireman soothed and spoke comforting words to Sonia and held her very close! Finally, the fire was extinguished.

The whole incident was reported on the evening news and the last images shown were very moving. Sonia was carried to the ambulance (still alive!). When the stretcher stopped next to the ambulance, the brave fireman who had sat in the car with Sonia, bent down and kissed her and then collapsed with exhaustion.

What an amazing true story! The fireman went against all his training and ran into the fire. He was already a hero (because all firemen are), but he revealed his heroic nature when he made the decision to run in and save her life. Heroism is not so much what you do, it is who you are! Even though common sense screamed "Don't run into the fire!" the hero inside him made him do it.

Imagine what would have happened if the fireman had said, "All I am paid to do is hold the hose." If he had said that, Sonia would have died. He could have walked away and said, "That'll do, I did enough."

But he didn't say, "That'll do!" He said, "I can do something about the situation and I won't be satisfied unless I do."

All too often at home, school, university, work and in our relationship with God, we use the words, "That'll do!" In other words what we are saying is, "I can't be bothered to do it any better – there's something else I'd rather do now!" If I was the devil, I'd try to help you say, "That'll do" for the rest of your life.

2. Don't believe the really weird Bible!

Imagine what the Bible would be like if the "that'll do" attitude ran all the way through it. In fact, let's imagine we've written a translation of the Bible called ...

The "That'll Do" International Version!

◆ Imagine what the Bible would be like if God had said, "That'll do" when He was creating the world. Every animal would have looked like a brown horse! I mean, horses are alright, but imagine trying to put a horse in a hamster cage! And how would you eat omelettes? Eggs come from a chicken's butt (nearly!). I am telling you, I ain't eating anything from a horses butt! The Bible would read something like;

◇ *"In the beginning God made the heavens and the horse! Now the earth was formless and void, but God created the horse and said, 'That'll do!' Now the horse was more crafty than any other horse. The horse whispered to Eve, 'Eat the apple, and while you're at it, give me some too, I am famished!' "*

53

OR

Jesus is the Horse of God?!

◇ (Read the real story in Genesis chapters 1 – 3 and John 1:29.)

◆ Noah could have said "That'll do" and immediately regretted building ... *"a canoe"* after it had been raining for a few days! It would read something like ...

◇ *"So Noah thought, 'Blow that for a pot of honey! I am gonna build a canoe. I'll put my wife and horse in it, but my sons are pretty good swimmers – they should be fine!' "*

◇ (Read the real story in Genesis 6 – 9.)

◆ Nehemiah could have said; "That'll do!" and only built half of the walls around Jerusalem! It would read something like ...

◇ *"Ouch! I'm tired of hitting my thumb with the hammer! Hey fellas, forget it! Let's play football instead, and when the enemies come, we'll challenge them to a game instead of defending the city!"*

◇ (Read the real story in Nehemiah 1 – 7:3.)

◆ David could have said, "That'll do!" and ran off when he saw that Goliath was bigger than a brick toilet. It would read something like ...

◇ *"Holy horse, I didn't think he was that big! Hey Saul, why didn't you tell me he was that big! How can he be so big? I have never seen anyone so big! I'm outta here!"*

◇ (Read the real story in 1 Samuel 17.)

◆ Daniel could have said, "That'll do!" when he was in the lions' den, and then let the lions eat him! (If you want to know what lions look like when they are eating, go to a youth camp sometime. Dinnertime is like feeding time in the lion pit, although – the lions probably have more etiquette! If you don't know what etiquette means, you have proven my point!) It would read something like ...

◇ *"Hey fellas, if you're gonna eat me, that's cool, but can we get this over with quick?"*

◇ (Read the real story in Daniel 6.)

◆ Hosea could have said, "That'll do!" and let his wife be a prostitute for the rest of her life. (That got your attention didn't it? And *NO*, I am not telling you where you can read about that one! And no I'm not gonna translate it either!)

◆ The four friends who carried the paralytic to Jesus could have said, "That'll do!" when they saw that the room was crowded, but they didn't. They started a demolition firm instead! It would read something like ...

◇ *"Hey Mack, we had a go, sorry to get your hopes up, but look on the bright side; there's a great kebab shop around the corner. Let's go get one – extra hot!"*

◇ (Read the real story in Mark 2:1–12.)

◆ Jairus could have said, "That'll do!" when his daughter was sick, but instead he went in search of Jesus. It would read something like ...

◇ *"Oh well, such is life!"*

◇ (Read the real story in Mark 5:21–43.)

◆ Peter could have said, "That'll do" and never have been the first man to water ski – barefoot! It would read something like ...

◇ *"Me? Walk out there? You're joking aren't you? I can't even walk straight on land, let alone out there on the water, in a storm!"*

◇ (Read the real story in Matthew 14:22–36.)

◆ Jesus could have said, "That'll do!" when he was in the garden of Gethsemane, but instead went all the way and died on a cross for you and me. Without that one act, life would be an absolute tragedy! It would read something like ...

◇ *"Me and pain don't do too well together. People aren't used to it where I am from. So Peter, you can die instead of me. Ok? Any questions?"*

◇ (Read the real story in John 19.)

◆ Paul could have said, "That'll do!" when the jailers were beating the stuffing out of him. He could have said, "I can't be bothered with this Jesus stuff!" and not written half of the New Testament. It would read something like ...

◇ *"Fair crack of the whip fellas, I am trying to write the Bible here, give me a moment! What was that? If I stop writing, you'll give me a time-share apartment in Crete? Deal! Thanks boys – I'm outta here!"*

◇ (Read the real story in Acts 16:6–40.)

◆ God could have said, "That'll do!" when it came to Him helping you. It could have read ...

◇ *"You are all a bunch of losers, save yourselves!"*

◇ But instead God,
   – "Devises ways so you can be in a relationship with Him" (2 Samuel 14:14).
   – "Reaches down from heaven, to pick you up and make you great" (Psalm 18).
   – "Died for us" (Romans 5:8).

And there are thousands more verses like it! And what about history? If people had said, "That'll do" in history, we wouldn't have:

• Peanut butter
• The light-bulb

- The internet
- Racial equality
- The Simpsons
- Football
- Cars
- McDonalds
- Playstations
- TV
- The chair you're sitting in
- The clothes you're wearing
- In fact, pretty much everything we see!!

So then, why, why, why, why, why do we say, "That'll do!" so much in life? Maybe the devil has something to do with it. If I was the devil, I would always be whispering to you, "That'll do", so that you always settled for average, instead of realising the power and creativity of God within you to do amazing things.

Imagine what your life would become if you aimed to do your best in everything and decided never to think or say, "That'll do!" Life would be awesome! You would be able to achieve absolutely everything God has ordained for your life.

There is an awesome verse in the Bible. Ephesians 3:20 says,

> *"Now to him* [God] *who is able to do immeasurably more than all we ask or imagine, according to his power that is at work within us."*

Did you get that? God's power is at work within you! So when you live by the "That'll do" code, you limit what you are really capable of doing.

3. Choose to live behind God's fences for your life!

I don't think the word "rules" best describes what God sets in place for us. I like to think of God's standards in terms of fences!

Think of it this way:

> Imagine Mike and Fiona are in love! They are gazing so much into each other's eyes that they don't realise they are walking straight towards a cliff edge. The drop from the cliff-top to the chasm below is about 600 feet. They keep walking closer and closer to the cliff edge, but they don't see it because they are so much in love.

Let me ask you a question. Which would you rather see?

- An ambulance waiting at the bottom of the cliff to take them away when they fall (and hopefully they'll be sewn back together), or
- A fence at the top making them aware of the potential catastrophe ahead?

Unless you are a sicko (you know, the type who actually likes the *Itchy and Scratchy Show* on the Simpsons), you will say, "I want the fence!"

That's exactly what God has done. So often we think the Bible is filled with rules, but actually they are fences. When it comes to sex, relationships, money, friends, priorities etc., God has written into the Bible a series of fences for each. We can jump the fences if we like, for example – have sex before marriage, go from one relationship to another, or be selfish with our money, but there is a lot of pain and hurt waiting on the other side of the fence.

God, because He loves us so much, builds fences and says, "Hey, stay back or you'll hurt yourself!" He doesn't do it because He is boring and wants your life to be the most miserable thing in the world. (Actually Jesus said He wants you to have the best life possible – John 10:10.) He does it because He is committed to your life being full of real satisfaction and fulfilment.

If I was the devil, whenever you get close to a fence, whether sex, money, relationships or whatever, I would constantly be whispering in your ear, "You don't really have to stay behind the fence – you can jump it if you like!" When it comes to God's "standard" for your life, I'd get you to compromise. Then I'd watch and laugh as you careered down the cliff wall and massively hurt yourself and others at the bottom.

Learn the lesson now – "Stay behind the fence!"

Pulling out tooth #3

Pulling out Tooth #3 is as simple as living to hear God say, "That'll do", because God's "That'll do", is much different from the devil's.

God's "That'll do" is best illustrated by the movie *Babe*. Babe the pig really wanted to be a "sheep-pig"! He couldn't understand that life for him was just about getting fat so one day someone could eat him. He wanted to be like the sheep-dogs who rounded up all the sheep when the farmer wanted. He watched the dogs and then decided one day he would do it! In fact, he got so good at rounding up the sheep that the farmer entered him into a sheep-dog contest and Babe (the pig) won! At the end of the movie, Babe sits down next to the farmer and the farmer says, "That'll do pig, that'll do!"

Now the movie isn't real. It's just a movie, but the farmer was saying far more than, "You were very average!" He was actually saying, "You did your best and that's what counts!"

It's worth living to hear God say, "That'll do – you did your *best* and that is what counts!" The Bible says that one day we will all stand before God face to face and we'll either hear Him say, "That'll do!" or "Go away – I never knew you." (You can read about it in Matthew 25:21.)

Your best, mixed with God's presence and power makes an awesome combination.

So, the next time you find yourself falling in line with the devil's version of "That'll do!" remember:

1. **Be the hero!**
2. **Don't believe the really weird Bible!**
3. **Choose to live behind God's fences for your life!**
4. **Live for God's "That'll do!"**

... and say to yourself: *Phew – that was close!* Then walk away with a smirk on your face thinking, *"Yep! There goes another tooth!"*

Coming up ...

First the dog, now the cat!

Making it real for you!

1. What does it mean to you to, "Be the Hero"?

   . . . .
   . . . .

2. Where do you need to be more of a hero?

   . . . .
   . . . .

3. There is no "That'll do" version of the Bible. In what areas of your life have you said "That'll do" that you know will actually "not do"?

   . . . .
   . . . .
   . . . .

4. Which fences do you struggle to stay behind?

   . . . .
   . . . .
   . . . .

5. Write a prayer asking God for His help to stay behind the fences you struggle with.

   . . . .
   . . . .
   . . . .

Someone once said ...

"Don't be so open-minded
your brains fall out."

Tooth #4

If I was the devil I would attempt to …

… distract you

Can I tell you one thing that really ticks me off? Bridges! Let me explain my frustration. There are times when I have either been driving my car or been a passenger in a car and we have approached a very scenic valley. The only way to get across the valley is by driving over a bridge.

So the scene is set: the sun is shining, the car is driving well, the CD player is thumping out some tunes, your friend is in the car with you and you have the opportunity to look out across a very beautiful part of the countryside. The only problem is this: you can't see a thing!!!

Why do the engineers who build bridges insist on building huge sidings or fences (of the non-see-through variety) on the sides of the bridge? As you look out from the bridge, hoping to get a view of the valley, all you see is a dirty grey/black wall.

It raises questions like, "What secret government initiative is taking place in that valley that they don't want us to see?" (Too much X-Files maybe?) "Did the hole-making machine (which makes holes in the walls for sightseers to check out the scenery) break down?"

I think the answer to the question is best found in something that happened outside my house once.

Curiosity killed the cat

In 1991 I was living in Manchester. Our house was on a main road which literally saw thousands of cars drive up and down it every day. One day I was walking home from college when I witnessed an accident. One car crashed into the back of another and before long the police were on the scene! I ran into the house, grabbed a bottle of coke and ran out to sit on the wall and watch what was going on. The events that were to follow made great viewing and since that time have made a great story to retell to friends.

The policeman was trying to make sense of two very irate drivers. Both were arguing their point, while the policeman was taking notes. As other cars approached the scene, they slowed down to negotiate around the crash, but also to have a good look at the situation (it's called rubber-necking!).

As the cars on the opposite side of the road were driving past, one of the car drivers looked so intently at the accident, he didn't notice that the car in front of him had stopped. Consequently, he drove into the back of the car in front. Now there was not just one accident, but two, right opposite each other!

The policeman yelled out, "I don't believe it!" and then added a string of obscenities aimed at the "dozy" driver who caused the second accident.

Now the road was congested with accidents, cars, police and interested onlookers. This was the best time I had had for ages. Soon, more police arrived to take notes on the situation and one began to direct traffic to and fro, in between the two crashes.

You'll never guess what happened next – or maybe you will. The traffic policeman was guiding some cars through the middle of the crash. One of the drivers thought the scene was hilarious and spent a little too much time laughing and staring at both of the crashes. She didn't realise that the car in front of her had stopped and ... crashed into the car in front of her!

By this time, I had fallen off the back of the wall laughing. With tears streaming down my face, I looked back over the wall to witness the policeman, onlookers, and the four other drivers who had been in the accident, stare in utter amazement and disbelief. In seemed like an eternity before anyone spoke and then simultaneously, two of the policemen began to swear whilst everyone laughed uncontrollably. Who would have imagined that three accidents could have taken place, on the same stretch of road, all opposite each other due to curiosity!

You know what they say about curiosity? *"Curiosity killed the cat."* My question is, "What did the cat want to know?"

So what caused the accidents? Well, the first accident is anyone's guess, but the other two were caused by curiosity. Curiosity led to distraction and distraction led to disaster!

If I was the devil, I would get you curious about things that are none of your business. I would tempt you with stuff that isn't necessarily evil (like sacrificing babies to idols or supporting Manchester United Football club), but things that would distract you from getting to know God.

The two big things the devil uses time and time again to distract you are relationships and peer pressure.

► *Relationships*
I often encourage the young people in our church not to let themselves get distracted by the old boyfriend/girlfriend saga! How many youth groups spend most of their time trying

to fix up, or talk about relationships in the youth? "She said this ... he did that ... I love you! ... I wish he hadn't finished with me and gone out with her!" And it goes on and on!

Someone once said to me that boys and girls dating and breaking off relationships is all part of growing up. I beg to differ! Why should teenagers have their hearts broken again and again! Surely that is not God's plan – surely there's a better way? Well, there is. Simply, don't make a big deal about relationships. Change the culture of the youth group so that it's cool to hang out together in big groups where everyone is everybody else's mate.

Incidentally, don't allow youth camps and conferences to be spoilt because of relationship sagas. Often good camps are ruined for young people because they meet, date and break up with someone whilst at the camp or soon after. Then, instead of remembering the week for God and the way He changed their lives, they only remember that girl or guy who broke their heart!

If I was the devil, I would get you involved in a super-intense relationship so that you spent more time focusing on your boyfriend/girlfriend instead of God. I would hope that you argue, fight, break up, get hurt – because while all of this is going on you'll find it hard to live for God's purposes.

▶ *Peer pressure*

There are four basic core values of every person. The need to *belong, believe, dream* and *achieve.* The first of these is what I want to really deal with right now.

Belong

Every one of us has the desire to be part of a group. (That's why young people hang out in posses or gangs. In winter in

England, you will see young people standing in the rain on a street corner, eating chips. Let's think about it rationally for a moment. The chips are wet, so are their socks and water is dripping off their noses. They are freezing to death, *but*, they are together and somehow that makes everything OK.)

We long to be missed when we are not at the regular events we attend and like to have someone phone us when we're not there.

We long to be welcomed when we arrive at a party and for people to make a big deal of you when we arrive. "Hey, Glyn's here! Now we can really start the party!"

Despite the fact that your friends help meet your first core value, they can also be responsible for putting pressure on you and at times are responsible for distracting you from what you know to be true and/or right! Things like:

- Discouraging you from going to youth group or church
- Pressuring you to have sex before marriage
- Challenging your integrity by encouraging you to steal or cheat
- Involving you in gossip or ridiculing others

If I was the devil, I would want you to be more interested in having cool friends and being a part of the "happening crowd", than pursuing your relationship with God. After all, everyone wants to be popular – so why sacrifice your popularity for the sake of being a Christian?

A great way to steal jewellery

A few years ago some thieves conjured up an amazing plan for stealing some jewels. They had been watching the jewellery store for a few weeks in an attempt to get to know the movements of all the staff. When the particular night came to break into the shop, they decided not to take anything away with them. They broke into the shop by removing the slates on the roof. They then slipped into the attic and removed some of the ceiling tiles. They de-activated the alarm and dropped into the shop. Instead of taking away the jewellery, they simply switched the price-tags. They found the expensive items of jewellery and changed the price tags with the cheap imitation jewellery and put the price tags from the cheap jewellery onto the expensive items. They had timed it just right, knowing that the next day all the experienced jewellers were away at a training day, meaning that the shop was left with "untrained" sales assistants. The burglars then climbed back into the attic, re-activated the alarm system, replaced the ceiling tiles, climbed out onto the roof, replaced the slates and went home.

The next day, the "untrained" sales assistants were excited. They sold an exceptionally high amount of the cheaper range of jewellery and assumed that when the boss came back from the training day, he would be really happy with their success.

The burglars were buying items of jewellery for $50, when they were actually worth $5,000. At the same time, couples who were not burglars in disguise were buying rings and necklaces at $10,000 dollars when actually they were worth $20.

That day, the burglars walked off with hundreds of thousands of dollars worth of jewels. A great idea, eh? Don't try it though, they got caught later!

That's a little bit like what I would do if I was the devil! I would switch the price tags. The things that God values the most, I would cheapen, and the things that I liked the best, I would make look attractive and appealing!

Let's see if we can make sense of this.

The car accidents on the road outside my house happened because the drivers were distracted. They didn't watch where they were going and they forgot the priorities of every driver: *to watch where you are going!* Instead, the drivers chose to focus on other things.

The theft of the jewels took place because the thieves changed the value of them. If the devil can get us to value and chase after that which is really not important, then he has successfully distracted us from the main event, which is living for God!

How can you make sure you don't get distracted from God's plans and purposes for your life?

1. Learn the lesson of Shadrach, Meshach and Abednego

King Nebuchadnezzar was a King in Babylon in Old Testament days. We read about him in Daniel chapters 1 – 4. In Daniel chapter 3, we read:

> *"King Nebuchadnezzar made an image of gold, ninety feet high and nine feet wide, and set it up on the plain in Dura in the province of Babylon. He then summoned the satraps, prefects, governors, advisers, treasurers, judges, magistrates and all the other provincial officials to come to the dedication of the image he had set up ... so* [they] *assembled for the dedication of the image ... and they stood before it. Then the herald loudly proclaimed ... 'as*

> *soon as you hear* [the instruments] *you must fall down*
> *and worship the image of gold.'"*   (Daniel 3:1–5)

Notice that the king didn't set up the statue in a cave, hole or in a gully. The Bible says he put it in the plain. This meant that it was in "plain view" of everyone. People living on the hill would open the curtains in the morning and see the statue. Everyone living in the plain could see the statue rising above the roof tops. You couldn't avoid the fact that the statue was there because wherever you were, you could see it!

Not only was it big, but it was also made of gold. Imagine the reflection of the sun on it. It would have been a spectacular sight!

Why was it so big? Because it was there to be *one big* distraction! Why was it so spectacular? Because it was there to be a *really big* effective distraction.

Shadrach, Meshach and Abednego (or "Shake-the-bed", "Make-the-bed" and "In-the-bed-we-go") are the heroes of the story. These three young guys loved God, but could easily have been distracted by all that was going on around them.

The king was so adamant that all the people would worship the statue that he issued a decree, *"Whoever does not fall down and worship will immediately be thrown into a blazing furnace!"* (Daniel 3:6). Now if that wasn't a good enough reason to worship the statue, I don't know what is.

The pressure was on these three guys to be distracted from their destiny of honouring God. Their distraction could have taken place in different forms:

- A spectacular sight (the statue was big and bright).
- Conformity (all the people were worshipping it).

- The loud declaration (what voice are you listening to?).
- The music (the best muso's and bands were playing).
- The king's threat ("I'll kill you if you don't").

They had every reason to be distracted from pursuing God and yet they said these words in Daniel 3:16–18:

> *"O Nebuchadnezzar, we do not need to defend ourselves before you in this matter. If we are thrown into the blazing furnace, the God we serve is able to save us from it, and he will rescue us from your hand, O king. But even if he does not, we want you to know, O king, that we will not serve your gods or worship the image of gold you have set up."*

Wow! Three young men who refused to be distracted! They saw the statue for what it really was: *an empty monument that when worshipped, would only cause their lives to crash and burn.* Shadrach, Meschach and Abednego refused to get sucked in by the hype!

The dictionary defines the word "hype" as "an empty reality". Hype is when something looks and sounds fantastic, but it doesn't live up to your expectations.

- Hype is spending £44 on a PS2 game that had rave reviews and amazing graphics (on the TV ad), only to discover it's worse than the game you invented on your computer when you were three-and-a-half years old.
- Hype is shooting for the moon, only to get as high as Blackpool Tower.
- Hype is seeing the girl of your dreams from a distance and then noticing her whiskers when you are close up.

- Hype is building a statue and getting everyone to worship it – but it's just a lump of metal!

Make a choice not to fall for the hype of what the world says is worth living for and giving your life for – no matter how glamorous it is! It will always lead you away from the stuff that really counts and the stuff of real value in life!

2. Choose not to go the way of the dumb!

The truth is that when you are distracted you end up doing dumb things. Take the time I had really bad hay fever. The doctor had prescribed some eye drops for me to take to alleviate the itchiness and redness in my eyes. When I say itchiness, that is an understatement. I wish I could have simply popped out my eyeballs, just to give them a good scratch.

One morning I slept through my alarm and woke up realising I had to leave the house in approximately 12 minutes if I was going to make it to the early morning staff meeting on time.

I had a mega-quick shower, threw on my clothes, brushed my teeth and was about to leave the house when I realised that I hadn't put in the eye drops. For a moment I contemplated what to do. It was only the third day of using the drops, so I knew I should put them in my eyes. I raced up to the bedroom, grabbed the little bottle that was on my bedside cabinet, sat on the floor in front of the full length mirror and started to shake the bottle to get a drop to fall into my eye.

During this whole time, I was only focused on one thing – getting out of the house so I could get to work. I began to shake the bottle: "Come on! DROP! DROP! DROP!" I was willing the drop to fall into my eye. It seemed to take a million years and then, just as the drop was forming, I realised something.

- This didn't *feel* like my eye-dropper bottle.
- This was a brown glass bottle. My eye drops are in a white plastic bottle.
- This has a green spout. My eye drops have a white spout on the bottle.

And as the drop fell from the bottle, I knew instantly what I had done. You see, next to the bottle on my bedside cabinet was a bottle of Olbas oil. Olbas oil is something you put on your pillow to help you breathe easy when you have a cold or hay fever. When the Olbas oil hit my eye I was *POLAXED*! Lying flat on my back I was screaming with agony. Now I *really* wanted to scratch my eyeballs!

The truth is, I put Olbas oil in my eyes because I was distracted from what I was doing. Instead of focusing on the eye drops, I was focused on getting out the front door. That moment of distraction led to *PAIN, PAIN, PAIN!*

The devil wants to distract us. If we let him, the result is: we do dumb things. I hear young people say:

- I don't know why I slept with that person
- I don't know why I went to that place
- I don't know why I did that thing
- I don't know why I said that thing
- I don't know how my life ended up like this

I do! You got distracted!

Pulling out tooth #4

Once when I was driving my dad's car through the suburbs of Sydney, I accidentally cut a guy up! Not literally you understand (I am not a serial axe murderer). I drove the car in front of his and if he hadn't braked, I would have been dead or he would have been dead or at the very least the cars would have been pretty messed up. The next few moments can only be defined as insanity. He got out of the car very angry and made his way towards me whilst gesticulating in a wild manner and clenching his fists. I thought to myself, "Self, this guy is going to eat you alive!" So I did what every other brave and courageous guy would do ... rammed the car into gear and took off. Thinking I had just escaped a near calamity (i.e. my head on a platter), I looked in my mirror to discover the guy was now chasing me. It was his car versus my dad's car. Fortunately dad had a good size engine and so the chase ensued (all within the speed limit of course)! At one point he overtook me and drove his car in front of mine. He braked slowly, forcing me stop to the car. When I did so, he again got out and this time I could tell he was seriously going to rearrange my face, so ... I reversed a little, drove around his car and took off. You guessed it – he came after me again!

I turned onto a dual carriageway and still he kept up the chase. Now travelling at a good speed in the outside lane (still within the limit), I took my one chance. Seeing a break in the central reservation and no oncoming cars, I did what I had seen the guys do in the *Dukes of Hazard* – I jammed on the hand brake and turned the wheel (N.B. don't try this at home!) Somehow, miraculously, I did a 180 degree turn and drove off back down the other side of the dual carriageway. It happened so quickly, the guy who was intent on squashing my nose missed his chance and had to carry on the other way. My heart was pounding, I couldn't believe what had just happened – it was like a movie.

And all because I cut him up! Hey, listen to what Paul says in Galatians 5:7, *"You were running a good race. Who cut in on you?"*

You see, if I was the devil, I would do everything I could to cut in on you and spoil your momentum, ultimately distracting you from pursuing God. When I cut in front of that guy in Sydney, he got mad. Hey, it's time to get mad at the devil! Don't let him distract you and get away with it, Fight back, get mad, make a decision not to be distracted!

How do you do that?

1. Remember "Curiosity killed the cat".
2. Don't fall for misplaced value (remember the jewellery store?).
3. Learn the lesson of Shadrach, Meshach and Abednego.
4. Choose not to go the way of the dumb!

Coming up . . .

The art of excuse making

Making it real for you!

1. If "curiosity killed the cat", what area have you been overly curious of, which you know will ultimately end up in disaster?

   . . . .

   . . . .

2. What three areas in life have you placed too much value on?

   . . . .

   . . . .

3. Hype is an empty reality. If you were to be honest, what "hype" did you fall for, only to be disappointed?

   . . . .

   . . . .

   . . . .

4. Distraction leads you to doing dumb things. On the scale below, identify how distracted (dumb) you have been by the things listed.

	Low				High
Relationships	1	2	3	4	5
Peer pressure	1	2	3	4	5
Image	1	2	3	4	5
Money	1	2	3	4	5
Music	1	2	3	4	5

Someone once said ...

"Age is of no importance
unless you are a cheese."

Tooth #5

If I was the devil I would help you to . . .

. . . find excuses

My best mate Lee really used to wind me up. He was eighteen months older than I, which meant that he was always faster, older, cooler and could always beat me in a fight. (That's different now of course – *now* I could whip him.)

I remember once he made me so mad that I jumped off my bike and ran at him. He just laughed and each time I went to grab him, he just pushed me to the ground. This made me even madder. The madder I was, the more haphazard I was. He just kept pushing me to the ground. I kept getting up until I realised I couldn't get him, so I ran inside and cried.

There was one time though (and I'm not proud of it) when I was really little, that I managed to give someone a black eye! I didn't mean to, it's just that my sister got in the way of the slipper that I threw at her. It connected with her eye and my dad's hand connected with my butt! When dad questioned me as to why I had given my sister a black eye, I replied, "I didn't mean to. I was just playing and she stuck her fat head in the way of the slipper!" At which point my dad's hand connected with my butt again.

Similarly when I discovered (with Lee) that fire likes dead leaves, causing us to burn down the ivy that grew up the side of his house, I found a great excuse as to why we had committed this act of arson.

Lee and I also managed to partake in *that* blowing up of a dog incident. (It always happened with Lee.) Again the excuses flowed between us.

The dictionary defines "excuse" as:

- *To seek to extenuate . . .* (Yep, I have no idea what that means either – let's try another one)
- *To free from blame or guilt*
- *To pass over; to overlook*
- *To pardon oneself*

The thing is, the excuses that I came up with for making bombs, lighting matches and giving black eyes were either lies *or* merely an attempt on my part to justify my shocking behaviour!

The truth? If I was the devil, I would help you to find the most creative excuses for your acting the way you do. Things like,

- *I thought it was OK to sleep with her. I just felt that since I was going to marry her anyway, it would be alright.*
- *I didn't mean to get drunk. My friends kept buying me drinks from the bar and you can't turn back a free gift!*
- *I didn't want to hurt anyone's feelings when I gossiped, but because it was the truth, I didn't think it was wrong!*
- *I know I didn't do my best, but what damage has it done really? I mean, people are starving in the third world and you're concerned that I did an average job!*
- *I knew I could get away with it because God is all-forgiving. I just thought I would do it and then God would forgive me!*

The devil has had thousands of years experience in making excuses. He has helped millions and millions of people to make excuses for why they did wrong and why things turned out the way they did.

There are four things that can help you overcome every excuse.

1. Look out for the oldest one in the book!

In Genesis chapter 3 we read about the fall of man. God made a perfect world and the devil did his utmost to ruin it. When Adam ate the fruit of the "tree of the knowledge of good and evil", he sinned. Adam's sin meant that we all became sinners. His one act of sin caused the whole of humanity to become sinful and consequently we are born as sinners. Pain, death, hurt, anguish, fear, loneliness and disappointment are all because of this one act. (Anyone want to have a chat with Adam when they get to heaven?) The good news is that in just the same way that sin entered the world through one man, salvation came to the world, by one man: Jesus Christ (read Romans 5:12–21).

Back in the beginning when Adam sinned, God questioned him in the same way my dad questioned me over the black eye incident. God said,

> *"Have you eaten from the tree I commanded you not to eat from?"* (Genesis 3:11)

Listen to what Adam says in reply:

> *"The woman you put here with me – she gave me some fruit from the tree, and I ate it."* (Genesis 3:12)

Classic! To make excuses is the oldest one in the book. Not only did Adam blame the woman, but inadvertently he blamed God too. He said to God, *"The woman **You** put here with me"*!

Our defence mechanism immediately tries to justify our behaviour and actions.

As a child I never willingly said, "Hey dad, I swore at lunch today when no one was looking – please discipline me!" I certainly didn't say "Dad, I threw the slipper at my sister because she upset me. I am truly sorry. I do hope you smack me for my actions!"

In actual fact, the reverse is true. Whenever we know we have done something we perhaps shouldn't have, we think of all kinds of excuses to squirm our way out of taking responsibility. Our desire not to take responsibility can best be summarised in two words,

RUN AWAY!

If I was the devil, I would help you to find excuses for sin. I would attempt to get you to believe them so much, that you became even more entangled in the mess you were in. Sin gives birth to more sin. Things go from bad to worse.

2. Recognise there will always be an excuse not to …

On the day my dad died, I was away from home. I was sure that in my diary it didn't say "dad is due to die today". It was something that was totally unexpected.

Within a week of my dad dying, my wife Sophia and I were due to pack all our belongings and move from

Australia to England to live and take up a youth pastorate in a church. Sophia and I needed to go to the British Embassy in the nation's capital, Canberra, to get her a visa so she could move to England. The day we were sorting out our future, our calling in God, our destiny, a spanner was thrown in the works – my dad died!

After hearing the news, we drove 3 hours back to Sydney, to the house where my family were grieving. Some days later, we went to view the body of my dad, on the same day as the funeral. As I stood in the funeral parlour, looking at my dad, this incredible hatred began to well up within me. If it wasn't for the devil and sin, my dad wouldn't be dead and we wouldn't have to be so upset at his loss. If the devil hadn't have tempted Adam and given him the gift of creative excuse making, then I wouldn't be standing in the funeral parlour.

At that moment I remembered what my Youth Pastor had taught me years before. He would say,

"Love God, Hate Sin!"

To be honest, I never understood it before, until that moment. From then on I began to direct hatred towards the devil and all the things he has on offer. When I am tempted to sin, and even when I do sin, I remind myself of the feeling I had that day when I looked at my dad.

You see, everything the devil has to offer anyone, always ends up leading to death, destruction and hurt. But God offers life! It's not a candy-coated poison-life like the devil offers – it's true life. Life with purpose, meaning, passion, focus and fun!

Don't hate people, politicians (they are people too), football teams etc. – hate sin and hate the devil!

There will always be a reason or an excuse why you can't achieve all God has for you. In this instance, my opportunity to find a reason not to go to England was staring me in the face – my dad had just died! I had delayed my move to England by about six weeks and it was time to get moving again with all God had for me there. I started reading 1 Timothy 5:16. It talks about family members being responsible for widows. I don't know if the devil helped me to find that verse (probably not), but he began to help me to use that as an excuse not to pursue the call of God for my life.

The question that raged inside my head was: *"How can I go to England, when my dad has just died? How can I leave my mum who is the widow that 1 Timothy 5:16 talks about?"*

Dad's death could have become an excuse for me not to move to England and follow God's plan. Thankfully, my mum helped me to see God's plan for my life. I delayed moving by six weeks, but some reading this book have delayed the call of God for your life indefinitely because of the excuses you have made.

3. Wake up or change your name!

There is a story about Alexander the Great which helps us to understand why we should not make excuses.

Alexander the Great had conquered the whole of the known civilized world by the time he was 23. At one particular campsite his men were sleeping in their tents, when he decided one night to walk around the site to check the morale of his men. As he approached one guard on duty, he found him sitting down, asleep. Alexander was very angry and kicked the soldier in the foot. When the guard looked up and saw Alexander, he feared for his life, because the penalty for sleeping on duty was death. Alexander the Great looked at this young soldier and demanded, "What is your name?" Sheepishly, the soldier replied, "Alexander, Sir." Alexander the Great paused for a moment and then said, "Well, either wake up and do your job, or change your name!"

Wow! You see the soldier carried the same name as the great general "Alexander the Great"! The challenge was either to live up to the reputation of the name Alexander, or change it to something else.

If we know Jesus as our Lord and Saviour, we carry His name about with us. The term "Christian" means "like Christ" or "little Christ".

We either need to wake up, accept our responsibility – that we have been called and equipped by God to do His work, or we should change our name.

4. Rely on your greatest friend and supporter

God doesn't expect us to do it alone. On our own, we will make excuses and will struggle and strive to be all we can be. But God's promise to us through the Bible is that He will help us if we let Him. Look at some of these verses in the Bible:

- *"In all your ways acknowledge him* [God] *and he will make your paths straight"* (Proverbs 3:6). God will help us if we simply acknowledge Him.

- *"The LORD is my strength and my shield; my heart trusts in him, and I am helped"* (Psalm 28:7). God simply asks us to place our full confidence in Him and He promises to help.
- *"So do not fear, for I am with you; do not be dismayed, for I am your God. I will strengthen you and help you: I will uphold you . . . "* (Isaiah 41:10). In other words, your excuse may be very real to you, but don't fear because God will help you!
- *" 'So we say with confidence, 'The Lord is my helper . . . ' "* (Hebrews 13:6).

You are not alone in your effort to beat the excuse trap. The devil may be creatively gifted at helping you find excuses why you can't achieve all God has for you. However, God is God and the devil doesn't even come close. Make the choice to let God help you to beat the excuse trap!

Pulling out tooth #5

It's one thing to make excuses, but what actually goes through your head when you look in the mirror last thing at night? The truth is that God wants us to live lives that are totally honest. He wants us to be honest with ourselves, each other and Him.

An excuse may be a little bit valid, or more probably it's a lie, but either way it doesn't help us to face the fact that we are ultimately responsible for the way we live.

So how do you beat the excuse trap?

1. Look out for the oldest one in the book! (Blame game!)
2. Recognise *there will always be an excuse* not to achieve everything God has for you.
3. Wake up or change your name.
4. Rely on your greatest friend and supporter.

Coming up ...

The day I nicked someone's sermon – word for word!

Making it real for you!

1. Think back – when you were younger, who did you
   usually blame when you did stuff wrong?

   . . . .

2. What excuse or excuses have you tended to use as a
   reason not to be the woman or man of God He has called
   you to be?

   . . . .
   . . . .
   . . . .
   . . . .

3. In what aspect of living for God do you really need to
   wake up and "live like God is watching"?

   . . . .
   . . . .
   . . . .

4. Write a prayer, asking God to help you to face life head
   on and not be an excuse maker any more!

   . . . .
   . . . .
   . . . .

Someone once said ...

"If at first you DO succeed,
try not to look astonished!"

Tooth #6

If I was the devil I would make you ...

... compare yourself to someone else

Let's face it! We have all tried to be someone else from time to time. Every guy has picked up a tennis racket or something else resembling a guitar and played "Air Guitar" whilst jumping up and down on the bed! What do you mean you don't know what air guitar is? Please allow me to enlighten you for a moment.

Hundreds of thousands of fans all chanting your name have gathered. You check downstairs to make sure mum, dad and especially your sister have left the house. You slowly mount the staircase, whilst imitating the sound of the screaming masses with two hands covering your mouth (this helps to create the sound of echo and mass hysteria). You slowly walk across the landing of your house, but realise that you left the tennis racket in the bedroom. You pause for a moment, the crowd continues cheering (because when you are making things up you can do whatever you want). You quickly slip into your bedroom (because at the moment, it's still just the bedroom). You turn on your bedside lamp (creates atmosphere) and then slip out of the room. Again you begin to make the sound of the masses, all chanting ("Glyn! Glyn! Glyn!") You give high fives to the rest of the band and then with dramatic poise, enter the bedroom, now

miraculously transformed (in your head) into a stage in front
of 100,000 people. They are screaming while you casually
wave to the highest terrace in the stadium (no point getting
too excited about it, you're used to this kind of acclaim).
Wiping the sweat from your brow, you climb up on top of
the bed head (realise that you forgot to position the mirror
correctly – quickly pause the crowds, because you can do
that – re-adjust the mirror so that you can see yourself
perfectly), climb back up onto the bed head and press play
on the remote control. The music thumps, you jump off the
bed head and start to play amazing guitar licks whilst your
fans scream adoringly. Everything is going well. The mirror
reveals you are *"looking good!"* and now you're lying on
your back whilst playing an amazing lead guitar solo ... At
this point, a huge light comes in from nowhere and your
sister is at the door, mocking you like the loser she thinks
you are!

Come on fellas, who's been there? Yep, I see all those
hands!

Hey girls, you may think that's kind of sad, but I
remember springing my sister once while she was using a
hairbrush as a microphone, pretending to sing in front of all
her fans.

So, the truth is, we have all, from time to time, wanted to
be someone else!

Maybe you've wanted to be like your best friend, a TV
personality or a movie star. I remember Thursdays in
primary school. My teacher was called Mr Head and I hated
Thursdays because Thursdays was affectionately called
" ... maths stuff"! (We all used to swap the words the other
way around, because basically we hated maths!) We hated it
because Mr Head took a certain amount of perverse pleasure

in presenting us with tests every Thursday. Our times tables had to be recited within a minute. Back then, I guarantee you it was really hard. I remember wanting to be my dad every Thursday. I wished I could have been in his shoes because,

1. I could drive his car to work, and
2. I wouldn't have to do "stuff m ... " I mean "maths stuff"!

I soon discovered that I couldn't trade places and live in dad's shoes (they were too big anyway).

If the devil is getting you to continually compare yourself with someone else, there are three sure-fire ways of making sure you don't fall into his trap and put him in his place.

1. Make the decision "You have got to be you!"

When I was 15, my family moved from Australia to Manchester. After a few weeks at the school, my teacher asked me to do the "God-talk" in chapel. I was instantly flattered and felt proud to be asked to do the job. After all, I was no longer the same "critter" who made bombs and blew up dogs. I had definitely changed.

When I got home that day, I suddenly realised, "Oh No! Doing the 'God-talk' means getting up in front of people and ... 'talking'." (Yes, I know I wasn't all that clever.) My revelation went further when I realised that in order to talk, I had to have something to say. I suddenly had that sinking feeling in the pit of my stomach. You know, the type of feeling you get when,

• Your dad says, "I want a word with you" or ...

- You get a letter to say your dentist appointment is next week, or ...
- You realise you just swam butt naked in front of your school ... you understand!

So now I am at home, scared about what to do and I suddenly remember something. The sinking feeling gives way to the feeling of "Yes! I have an idea!"

David Meece was a singer songwriter from America (yep, I'll admit there were times when I was him, playing air guitar – although he played piano, which wouldn't really work, because you couldn't play air guitar with a piano because it's too heavy, and ... never mind!). On one of his albums he did a 7 minute preachy bit and so I decided I would nick it!

I wrote it out word for word, practised and practised and then came the big day.

I woke up early, had that sinking feeling again, but put on David Meece and heard the way he delivered it one last time. I had a shower and played a little bit of air guitar. Yep, I was looking good. Now it was time.

I rode my bike to school (looked a bit wind-swept when I got there, but it gave me that rugged/unkempt look). I walked into the chapel service and was introduced to the school. There was applause and instantly I was taken back to air guitar land! Yep, I had been here before.

I stood up to talk and it was going really well. People were laughing in all the right places, as well as oohing and aahing in all the right places too. This was good! But, it all started to go pear-shaped when I mentioned that in 1968 I was driving my Buick down the main highway in Chicago (or words to that effect), and you could see people's minds begin to do some mental arithmetic. Their heads probably told them something like this,

- "Glyn, you weren't born in 1968!"
- "Glyn, you've never been to America!"
- "Glyn, you can't even drive a car!"

From that point on, I had *really* gained their attention. They knew I had made everything up. They knew I had copied someone else. In fact, my teacher said, "Glyn, well presented, but perhaps it would be better if you were yourself and stopped trying to be like someone else!" I was so embarrassed!

Fifteen years later, I still struggle with being like someone else from time to time. Even as a full-time Pastor there are still times when I would love to be like someone else!

After taking up the Youth Pastorate in Sheffield, I was invited to speak in another country. I arrived on a Monday and did a full week of schools work and was gearing up for the big youth event on the Friday night. My time in the schools had gone really well, but all week someone was putting big pressure on me! The people who had invited me across to that country so wanted me to put on a "big performance" at the Friday night youth event. Their words went *something* like this:

- "Wow Glyn, you should have seen the last youth event. It was incredible. 53 people became Christians."
- "The time before last we had Jeff preach (not really his name). He was amazing. He was funny, everyone laughed their heads off and when he preached the Word, 72 became Christians."

- "Before that Matt preached (again not really his name). We have never seen anything like it. He raised people from the dead. We even killed people, just so he could raise them back to life again."
- "But Glyn, we only want you to be you – no pressure!"

OH SURE! NO PRESSURE – YOU'RE KIDDING ME AREN'T YOU? WHY DON'T YOU JUST GET THE NOOSE AND HANG ME NOW, YOU PEASANTS!!!

Of course, I didn't reply like that, but I did cast my mind back to the bomb I had made, trying to recall *what the ingredients were!*

As Friday night approached, the sinking feeling grew! When I had to stand to preach, I thought, the only way to pull this off is to be like Matt! So I tried and guess what? I had the same feeling that night that I had had when I was 15, speaking in the chapel service in my school! It was simply awful. No-one responded to the gospel (actually the people who hosted the event put up their hands to respond, just because they felt sorry for me and just so I could say, "I see that hand!"). I felt like a fraud!

On both those occasions and other times in between, I had fallen into the trap of comparing myself to someone else. I thought the only way I could do a good job was to be like someone else. It didn't work the first two times, or any time since.

If I was the devil, I would be telling you that,

- Your butt is bigger than your friend's.
- You are not as popular as your best mate.
- You are not as fashionable as the others.
- You are not as talented and gifted as the rest.

- ... and every other comparison trap you have ever fallen into ...

If I was the devil I would put pressure on you to be like someone else, because if you try to be and act like someone else, then I have successfully,

- Robbed the world of you.
- Deprived the world of your answer to their questions.
- Stolen your uniqueness from you.
- Frustrated you.
- Taken you away from you the power and equipment God has designated for you to fulfil His purposes!

2. You have to understand what "your gift" does for you

Guess what? Three months later the people who hosted this event rang me back. They said, "Glyn we'd like you to come back in six months to speak at the event again" – to which I flatly replied, "Why?" Let's face it, I hadn't done a good job, I couldn't understand why they wanted me back. Were they mad?

They replied, "We figured you had an off day!" Cheers! I reluctantly, after trying to put them off, said "yes." As the day to fly to that country fast approached, I had that sinking feeling again, when out of the blue a friend rang me. He said, "Glyn, I was praying for you today and God gave me Proverbs 18:16 for you." I thanked him, hung up the telephone and opened the Bible to that verse. It read,

> *"A gift opens the way for the giver*
> *and ushers him into the presence of the great."*

My life changed in a flash! Let me dissect this verse for you.

Back in Old Testament days, whenever a king or one of the leaders of a nation wanted to visit the king of another nation, he would send an envoy with gifts. In fact this happened in 1 Kings chapter 10. The Queen of Sheba visited Solomon. Before she arrived, she sent a huge caravan full of gifts for the king. The Bible says that no one had ever brought so many gifts to Solomon before. The very act of presenting Solomon with gifts meant that the king would look favourably towards her and the door would be opened so the Queen of Sheba could have access to see King Solomon.

We don't do this sort of thing today, but the spiritual truth of this is still very real. God has gifted you with abilities and talents. Please understand He has "gifted" you. In other words He has placed gifts within your life.

- Spiritual gifts (1 Corinthians 12)
- Natural gifts
- Ascension gifts (Ephesians 4)
- You are actually a "gift" too.

So whenever you walk into a situation, or embrace a doorway of opportunity, you have to realise that the gifts within you go immediately before you (just like the Queen of Sheba's gifts to Solomon) and go on to give you access *"into the presence of the great."* (That's the great unexpected situations you find yourself in, and you hear yourself say, "Wow! How did I end up here?")

Let me explain this further by telling you what happened when I went back to that country to do the youth event. The plane was coming into land in that nation's capital. I had a great sense of relief when I realised that all I had to do was be myself. I didn't have to be David Meece, Jeff or Matt! Just me! In fact, I was flying into that country because I *was* me and because the gift of God in my life opened the door of opportunity for me to be there.

As I stood to preach at the youth event, I was relaxed in the fact that I was me *and* I preached brilliantly. Loads of young people responded to the gospel. Afterwards, the people who put the event on began to say, "You're the best we have ever had. We're going to tell Matt and Jeff that you were better than them and we'll tell the next guy about you too." I said, "You don't need to tell them anything like that! Just let them be themselves and don't compare, especially in front of the next guy."

I'll admit, I got upset with this couple. Why? Because they were partly responsible for encouraging the attitude of "comparison".

You don't get the opportunities you are given (and will be given in the future) because you are *like someone else.* You have the opportunities you have because you are *YOU*, and the gift of God within you has made way for you. God does not want you to be someone else – He wants you to be you! No power or authority can result from me trying to be you, or you trying to be me. (The devil knows that and that's why he tries to get you to compare yourself to others so often.) You are created by God to be *YOU*, with your unique gifts and abilities! Don't deprive the world of *YOU* any more. Be you and let the gift of God create room for you!

3. Know how the anointing works!

The word "anointing" used to confuse me! For a while I thought the anointing was,

- Something only preachers got
- A shiver down your liver
- A paranormal feeling that made you fall over
- Something reserved for those only closest to God.

At Bible College I did a dissertation (in other words a very long essay with loads of information, filled out with lots of waffle so you can complete your 25,000 word target). For my dissertation I decided to study the word "anointing" to discover what it really meant and came to the conclusion that the anointing is two things,

1. "To be set apart by God"
2. "The power and equipment to do God's will"

So get this. God set you apart (first meaning) since before time began (Jeremiah 1:5) and created you with a specific purpose in mind. He would be a cruel God if He asked you to do something that you were incapable of doing. So He anoints you (second meaning), or "gives you the power and equipment" to do everything He asks of you. This is absolutely brilliant. You see, He doesn't anoint you or empower you to be like anyone else. The moment you try, God says, "Oh well, you do it alone!" But when you stop comparing and decide to be you, He empowers you to not only do it, but do it *well*!

How do you get "the anointing"?

It's simple really. Just live the life you believe God wants you to live. As you live a life of holiness and righteousness (in other words living right before God) and you allow God to guide you at times when you are making big decisions, i.e. which college/university course to do, which job to take etc., you will find that God will give you peace about which decision to make. Gradually you will discover what God has set you apart for.

Then, as you begin to follow that path for your life, God supernaturally enables you to do what you need to do (you still have to work hard though!).

Too many people get hung up on having "the anointing". Don't do that, just live every day like God is watching and let Him into your daily routine through prayer and Bible reading. Before long, you will find that God's empowering of you is just happening because you are a supernatural person living life for a supernatural God!

Be you – not your friend! God will empower that!

Pulling out tooth #6

Your "success" is not measured by how well you are doing in comparison to someone else. You measure your "success" by how well you are doing in comparison to what God has asked you to do! So then, *why be like someone else? You play **you** much better!*

Quick recap: How do you stop the comparison?

1. Remember, "air guitar" is not real!
2. Make the decision, "You have got to be you!"
3. Understand what your "gift" does for you.
4. Know how the anointing works in your life.
5. Re-evaluate what you compare yourself to.

Hey, no more comparison! And if the devil whispers in your ear again, tell him to compare himself to God – Ha, watch him run!

Coming up ...

The day I burnt the church pews!

Making it real for you!

1. Recount your "air guitar" story, or a similar make-believe world where you stepped into someone else's shoes.

   . . . .
   . . . .
   . . . .

2. Who do you continually wish you could be and why?

   . . . .
   . . . .

3. How does knowing your "gift makes way for you" make you feel about yourself?

   . . . .
   . . . .
   . . . .

4. How does knowing how the "anointing" works make you feel about life?

   . . . .
   . . . .
   . . . .

5. Make a conscious effort to measure yourself against what God has called you to do in life and not how and what "others" are doing!

Someone once said ...

**"Everything happens for a reason
... God needs a laugh."**

It's true – look at your best mate!!!

Tooth #7

If I was the devil I would make you ...

... take the easy option

Why do something the hard way, when you can do it the easy way? In one particular adventure movie, one of the characters says, "Do you ever do things the easy way?" She replied, "Never, I wouldn't want to disappoint!" Even though that's a great sound bite, the truth is that we usually always take the easy option. I'll prove it:

- Do you deliberately choose the longest queue in the shop? No
- Do you deliberately look for the attendant at McDonalds who has "trainee" on their badge? No
- Do you deliberately walk to school/work rather than drive or take the bus? No
- Do you get into the car through the window? No
- Do you put your clothes on in the dark? No

We are usually on the look out for the quickest, timesaving, "get it now" type of activity. Patience may be a virtue, but we live in a time when there isn't much of it! Someone once said; "God grant me patience and I want it now!"

The thing is, Jesus didn't take the easy option. Let's see if we can record what He did and how it could have been easier ...

- He came to earth! It could have been easier – He could have sent an angel.
- He lived as a man. It could have been easier – He could have come as a woman! (joke).
- He was whipped, beaten and crucified. It could have been easier – He could have just been shot!

The amazing thing is, Jesus doesn't give us the easy option in following Him. In fact, He says that there is a cost to following Him. Jesus talks about this in Luke 14:25–27:

> *"Large crowds were travelling with Jesus, and turning to them he said: 'If anyone comes to me and does not hate his father and mother, his wife and children, his brothers and sisters – yes, even his own life – he cannot be my disciple. And anyone who does not carry his cross and follow me cannot be my disciple'"*

OUCH! I don't know about you, but that sounds a little bit harsh!

You see the truth is that following Jesus does require a cost on our part. It's definitely not the easy option! Salvation is free, but to follow Jesus costs us something.

Jesus often made it difficult for people to follow Him. Look at these verses:

- *"Another disciple said to Him* [Jesus], *'Lord, first let me go and bury my father.' But Jesus told him, 'Follow me, and let the dead bury their own dead.'"* (Matthew 8:21–22)
- *"Go, sell your possessions ... then come, follow me ..."* (Matthew 19:21)

- *"How hard it is for the rich to enter the kingdom of God! Indeed it is easier for a camel to go through the eye of a needle than for a rich man to enter the kingdom of God"* (Luke 18:24–25)

We have to recognise that there *is* a cost to following Jesus.

If I was the devil, I would be encouraging you to take the easy option because Christianity is "too tough!" (N.B. The easy route isn't the easy route in the long run! It's a question of eternity and where you will spend it.)

It is tough being a Christian! But can you safeguard yourself to make sure you don't take the seemingly "easy route" when it comes your way? There are five things to remember to make sure you carry on in your God-given destiny.

1. Know the facts about counting the cost

Let's have a look at the verses in Luke again;

> *"Large crowds were travelling with Jesus, and turning to them he said: 'If anyone comes to me and does not hate his father and mother, his wife and children, his brothers and sisters – yes, even his own life – he cannot be my disciple. And anyone who does not carry his cross and follow me cannot be my disciple.' "*

Look at what the cost of following Jesus is:

▶ *You have to go against popular opinion*
Crowds are led by crowds. In London once, there was a crowd. Because there was a crowd, others joined the crowd

to see what the crowd was doing. Still more joined the crowd, until there were thousands all together. Do you know what the crowd was doing? Nothing! Everyone was there wondering why everyone else was there!

A few years ago, I sat in the great amphitheatre in Ephesus where the riot took place in Acts 19. Check out these great verses:

> *"Soon the whole city was in an uproar. The people seized Gaius and Aristarchus, Paul's travelling companions from Macedonia, and rushed as one man into the theatre. Paul wanted to appear before the crowd, but the disciples would not let him. Even some of the officials of the province, friends of Paul, sent him a message begging him not to venture into the theatre. The assembly was in confusion: Some were shouting one thing, some another. **Most of the people did not even know why they were there.**"* (Acts 19:29-32)

You see, the crowd was there, but didn't know *why* they were there. Luke 14 says, *"Large crowds were travelling with Jesus."* Jesus wasn't impressed by large crowds. He knew that the crowds were fickle. He knew one day they loved Him and the next they would shout, "Crucify Him!"

The crowds come and go; they believe one thing and then another. They put pressure on you to do one thing one day and another thing the next. The point is, that the crowd will more often than not, attempt to make it difficult for you to follow Jesus by pressuring you to follow the current hype of the day.

Usually, the crowds you will find yourself in the most (i.e. at school, college etc.), will not be jammed with Christians.

Because of that there's "peer pressure" to lower your standards on integrity, honesty, holiness, morality and many other issues that arise. When you refuse to go with the crowds' opinion because you know in God's eyes that it is wrong – you count the cost – because it often leads to ridicule, fear and even embarrassment.

▶ *Others have to count the cost when you do*

Jesus said, *"If anyone comes to me and does not hate his father and mother, his wife and children, his brothers and sisters . . . "*

Jesus is not saying that I have to literally "hate" my wife Sophia and my children, Georgia and Jaedon. He is not saying that I have to *loathe* (cool word) my mum. But He is recognising that when you count the cost of following Jesus, you make others count the cost too. Let me explain what I mean.

When I was 12 years old, I said "yes" to God. Basically, anything He wanted me to do in life, I said "yes!"

In 1996, my wife Sophia and I said goodbye to our families in Australia (my father had just died) and we moved to Sheffield, England. In that time, we have had two children and have seen and been a part of exciting things. The problem is, we don't get to share those things with our parents, brothers and sisters. They live on the other side of the world. Saying "yes" means that we have to count the cost of following Jesus every day because we cannot see our family whenever we want. It also means that our families have had to count the cost too, because they can't see us every day as they would like to. Mum can't wake up and say, "I'd like to see my granddaughter or grandson today," because she can't. She lives 16,000 miles away!

You see, when you follow Jesus, you make others count the cost. Your friends will say, "You are not like you used to be. You used to get drunk with us. You're not much fun any more." Parents may encourage you not to go to church or youth group or even Bible College, because they don't understand what you have found in God. They put pressure on you to do other things. I am amazed by the amount of times I have heard parents talk so badly about their kids being part of a church, that the only conclusion I can come to is that they are happier when their children are getting drunk and sleeping around, rather than being in the church. *WHY?* Because they don't understand what the whole thing is about. They are counting the cost of you following Jesus.

Jesus talks about hating family and friends because sometimes they can hold us back from going all out for Him. Jesus says: "Hey, put what I think before the opinion of others – especially those closest to you."

▶ *Hardship and suffering is the road to success*
Look again at what Jesus says: *"... anyone who does not carry his cross and follow me, cannot be my disciple."*

The cross that Jesus carried was heavy! Not only that, it also dug into the open wounds on His back. When Jesus spoke about carrying the cross, He wasn't speaking about something easy. He was speaking about something that conjures up the image of pain and hardship.

Jesus is telling us here to expect hardship in following Him.

- It's hard when your friends make fun of you for being a Christian.
- It's hard when a teacher at school ridicules your faith in God.

- It's hard when your friends are going somewhere to have fun, when you know it's not God's ideal place for you to go.
- It's hard to stand up for God, when things seem to be falling apart around you.

The gospel was never, "Come to Jesus and everything will be a bed of roses." He does not promise an easy time, but He does guarantee a life filled with purpose, hope, destiny and completeness. Hardship is the road to success.

In verse 35 of Luke 14 Jesus says, *"He who has ears to hear, let him hear."* In other words Jesus is saying, *"Hey, what I have said about it costing you something to follow Me is absolutely true. Really listen to Me because even though salvation is free, discipleship costs you everything!"*

We take the easy option in everything in life, but there is no easy option with God. For success, you have to be prepared to give up everything for Him.

2. Get to grips with the devil's plan

We are so used to taking the easy road that we expect Christianity to be easy too. We expect the devil to say, "Hey, carry on living for God, pursuing destiny and destroying my kingdom." But the Bible says we are in a war! There is a war of two kingdoms, two worlds and the war is over the destiny of our souls. We are smack bang in the middle of the war!

Ephesians tells us, *"For our struggle is not against flesh and blood but against . . . the spiritual forces of evil in the heavenly realms"* (Ephesians 6:12).

The fact is, *YOU ARE IN A WAR!* You can't pretend it's not happening; you can't choose to be neutral. The war is raging right now and your soul is at stake. Because the devil doesn't want you to pursue God, he is doing all he can to persuade you to do otherwise. His ploy is this: "Young people are so used to taking the easy option, I'll just give them easy options when the pressure is on to be a Christian. I'll make it easier for them not to be a Christian!"

It is tough being a Christian. Tough yes, but not impossible. In Luke 18, in response to Jesus' comments about how difficult it is for a rich person to be saved, the people say, " 'Who then can be saved?' Jesus replied, 'What is impossible with men is possible with God' " (Luke 18:26–27).

God is on your side! You don't battle alone. He is with you every step of the way. In the middle of the most intense pressure, when you feel like giving up on your destiny in God, He is one prayer away. When you ask Him for help, He does something on your inside and gives you the "supernatural" confidence to face what you need to face.

3. Learn not to wait for the sale!

Do you like sales? I do. I like the idea of buying something for less than it is worth. I love buying a jacket that was 75 quid, but is now 20 quid. There is a great sense of satisfaction in that. The idea of a sale is you get more for less. But we sometimes try to do the same with God. We say, "Hey God, I want everything You have to offer me, but let me strike a bargain. Can I have everything You want for me, but get it on the cheap?"

God replies, "No sale! This is the way it works: I'll do you a trade. I'll take your life and everything you have to offer Me: sin, mess, filth, self etc., and I'll give you My life in place of yours – righteousness, wholeness, contentment etc." There's no sale, no waiting for the cheap option, it's a straight swap – your life for His. It will cost you everything, you have to give Him *every* part of your life!

Sometimes sales are very expensive! There have been times when I have seen an item of clothing that I have really liked, but thought "I'll wait for the sale!" By the time the sale came along, all the items I was interested in were gone and I never did get that t-shirt I really liked.

Some Christian young people are waiting for the sales, waiting for God to strike a better deal, a cheaper deal on their part. But God says there is no sale – it will cost you everything to get everything! Some young people are waiting for the day when they can have God without having to pay the cost of following Him. They put off committing their life to Jesus, waiting for sale day. Unfortunately for many, they will discover that just like my t-shirt, salvation and Christianity is not a sale item. They end up with nothing. Life wasted!

Let's be honest, what have you got to lose? If there is no easy option for God, then why wait for the sale when you know now there isn't going to be one?

4. Choosing not to go for easy option pays off in the end

My family moved to England when I was fifteen because my dad had accepted an offer from a church where the elders had said, "We'll do anything you want, we just want to grow!" Six months later, it was apparent that despite their letter stating they wanted to change, they didn't really want to. After six months people still sat in the same chairs and the elders were creating havoc with my dad's plans to embrace change and grow the church.

One day, my dad encouraged me to take a day off school (which was brilliant, because usually he was making me go) and we went up to the church building. I soon found myself helping him to carry out the wooden pews onto a spare plot of land next to the church. We also carried out the huge oak lectern. Everything was piled high. Some chairs we gave away, but the rest were sitting in a pile. My dad then poured some petrol over the chairs etc. Then he gave me some matches and said, "Here, you light it!" I said, "Why me?" and he replied, "So I don't get into trouble!" So, smiling, remembering my expertise with fire and bombs as a child, I set fire to the pile of chairs. It was a great bonfire.

The next week, 60 people came to church and 30 left, but it was the start of change. My dad received angry letters from people who had sat in those chairs for many years. But the truth was that most people were more attached to their chairs than the advancement of the gospel. They didn't really want to count the cost!

It was a difficult time for my mum and dad as people left the church. But dad persevered with renovating the building and commencing relevant programmes and ministries for the people of the area. The church soon turned a corner, people got saved the youth group was thriving. The church began to boom.

It wasn't an easy option, but it was the right option. Walking the hard road meant turning our backs on the opinions of people. Jesus had to do it and it became the road to success and victory.

5. Choose the narrow gate

In Matthew 7:13–14 we read;

> *"Enter through the narrow gate. For wide is the gate and broad is the path that leads to destruction, and many enter through it. But small is the gate and narrow the road that leads to life and only a few find it."*

The opinion of others (and especially the devil) can hold you back from living all out for God. The pressure to take the easy option is great, but the easy option, or as the Bible calls it, *"the wide road/gate"* leads to destruction. Do you know that the narrow road/gate leads to life? Not following the opinion of others, but living for God's opinion is what counts. The narrow gate is simply the choice to follow Jesus Christ. The decision to follow Jesus is the turning point in everyone's life.

The road to eternal life passes through a narrow gate. The narrow gate is the choice to follow Jesus Christ as your Lord and Saviour. Jesus said, *"I am the way and the truth and the life. No one comes to the Father except through me"* (John 14:6). The narrow gate is not filled with options. There is only one choice – to follow Jesus. In John 10:10 Jesus says, *"I have come that* [you] *may have life, and have it to the full."*

The truth is simple: the road and the gate may be narrow, but as you count the cost of following Jesus and turn your back on the devil who says, "take the easy option" you'll discover that the narrow gate leads to a wide, abundant, exciting lifestyle where "air guitar" and "blowing up dogs" pales into insignificance.

Pulling out tooth #7

Tough chapter? Let me remind you of how you can make sure you don't take the "easy option":

1. Know the facts about counting the cost.
2. Get to grips with the devil's plan.
3. Learn not to wait for the sale!
4. Remember that choosing not to go for the easy option pays off in the end.
5. Choose the narrow gate.

Hey – don't go the easy option that leads to destruction, count the cost, because that is the way that really leads to *LIFE*!

Coming up …

Time is tickin' away!

Making it real for you!

1. Rate yourself on this "counting the cost" scale. How well are you counting the cost?

	Low				*High*
Going against popular opinion	1	2	3	4	5
Making others count the cost	1	2	3	4	5
Accepting hardship and suffering as the road to success	1	2	3	4	5

2. How has the devil given you the "easy opt out" over the past few years?

   . . . .
   . . . .

3. In what areas have you held back from God? How can you better give all of yourself to God, instead of waiting for the cheap option?

   . . . .
   . . . .
   . . . .

4. Write a prayer, asking God to help you to hold fast and not take the easy route when the devil offers you the opportunity.

   . . . .
   . . . .

Someone once said ...

"I have the body of a GOD –
Buddha."

Tooth #8

If I was the devil I would tell you ...

... you've got lots of time!

(Here's a quick chapter to prove otherwise!)

When you were 8 years old, anything over the age of 15 was really old! My sister Sian is six years older than I and forever it felt like she was the same age as my mum and dad, which clearly was not the case, but when I was 10, it felt like it!

When I was 8, Lee (remember the one who dated Fiona!) and I sat on the curb-side of the road. It was a hot day, probably 35 degrees Celsius. The sun was so hot that the tarmac on the road was melting and bubbling. As we were popping bubbles of tarmac, we started to dream about what the world would be like when we were old enough to drive. We were smart 8-year-olds and guessed that if we couldn't drive until we were 17, that meant we had nine years to wait.

Lee told me the type of car he wanted to drive and not being one to be out done I said, "Lee, that's nice, but by the time we drive, cars won't have wheels, they'll have wings and they'll fly!" We lay back on the grass, staring up at the clouds and whilst making out shapes in the clouds (Hey, there's your mum's head – yeah – there's an elephant – Oh, no ... it's still your mum's head!) we began to dream about flying cars and life nine years later.

Twenty-three years later and that day seems like yesterday. At the time, it felt like it would take forever for nine years to pass by. In actual fact, nine years didn't take long at all. Since that day, I have lived in Australia twice and England twice. I got married, had two children, lived in two different houses, owned two different cars etc. Time has flown by. When I was a kid I believed that time lasted forever. When I was a teenager, I believed what every teenager believes: "I'll live forever." Now as a Pastor, having taken marriages, funerals and dedications, I think I am a little wiser (not much though) and I realise, "I won't live forever" (in this body – although I wish I could – it's almost perfect!) and yes, time flies!

I know people who have said, "I'll become a Christian later – I have loads of time!" Part of being young is all about thinking you are immortal. I hate to spoil the party, but it's not quite true!

Someone once said, "The road to hell is paved with good intentions." I think he meant that many people who are spending an eternity in hell, thought they would have another opportunity to give their lives to God, or to commit themselves to serving the purposes of God. They always had the intention of getting their lives right with God, but kept putting it off for another day.

One thing you don't have is "yesterday" and you don't have "tomorrow", but you do have "now"! The power of the decisions you make today affect what your life will be like tomorrow. If I was the devil, I would help you to put off making important decisions which affect eternity and the great purposes of God for your life. In actual fact, if I was the devil, I would be whispering in your ear,

- You've got lots of time!
- You've got lots of time to get your life right with God – so live a little first!
- You've got lots of time to start going to church and pursue the kingdom of God.
- You've got lots of time to become boring like all the other Christians and do nothing exciting with your life.
- You've got lot's of time to apologise to your friend.
- You've got lots of time to forgive your parents for what they did.
- You've got lots of time …

Ecclesiastes says, "There is time for everything," but there isn't an endless supply of it. You've now got even less time than when you started this chapter! Time is going … going … soon to be gone!

The greatest thing you can do with your time is found in Ephesians 5:15–16. It reads, *"Be very careful then, how you live – not as unwise but as wise, making the most of every opportunity, because the days are evil."*

The King James Version of the Bible translates "making the most of every opportunity" as *"redeeming the time."* The greatest thing you can do with time is to "redeem" it. *Redeem* is a legal term which originally meant, "to buy a slave with a view to freeing them". Equally, to redeem the time means to free it from things that waste it and use it to your best advantage. So what are some ways to redeem your time?

1. Remember your Creator!

Ecclesiastes 12:1 says, *"Remember your Creator in the days of your youth."*

Youth is the age of "immortality". We never really think about death, because it seems so far off. There is a sense that we will "live forever!" Of course the truth is quite the reverse. The longer you live, the more you realise that young people die too!

Remembering your Creator in your youth saves you from the "silly season". In Luke 15 you can read the story about the "Prodigal Son" – a young man who threw off all restraints and ran to indulge himself in a life of pleasure. In the end that pursuit cost him everything and when he was at his lowest, the Bible says, *"he came to his senses"* (Luke 15:17). He had spent a silly season losing everything he had worked for in selfish pursuit, causing heartache and distress along the way. He forgot his Creator! Choosing to remember your Creator, God, will cause you to live the life of destiny God has for you and will save you from the distress that selfish ambition causes.

Every moment wasted is a moment's delay in picking up God's awesome dream for your life. No more silly seasons! Live the dream – remember your Creator!

2. Remember the comeback King is coming

Some sportsman make so many come-backs that when they say they are retiring, it's hard to know whether it's true or not. But Jesus, is the comeback *KING!*

- King Herod tried to kill Him as a baby – but He came back!
- The devil tried to tempt Him – but He came back!
- The Jews denied Him – but He came back!
- The devil killed Him – But He came back!

- At the moment He's waiting for His final comeback and it will be *HUGE!* (Read 1 Thessalonians 4:13–18.)

We have to be on the lookout, ready for Him, because the truth is, Jesus could come back today! Each moment that passes is a moment closer to the return of Jesus. He is coming back to take us to Heaven with Him! He's coming soon. Are you ready?

3. Number your days

A few years ago, I had the opportunity to hear a great sermon on Psalm 90:12. It says, *"Teach us to number our days ... "* In the sermon, the preacher did exactly that, he numbered his days, so I thought I would do the same:

I was born on day	1
I became a Christian on day	912
I went to School on day	1,825
I got filled with the Holy Spirit on day	4,380
I was baptised in water on day	4,410
I went to High School on day	4,745
I moved to England on day	5,505
I graduated from College on day	6,570
I moved back to Australia on day	7,330
I met Sophia on day	7,360
I went to Bible College on day	7,695
I got engaged on day	8,515
I graduated from College on day	8,716
I got married on day	8,730
My dad died on day	8,790
I moved to Sheffield on day	8,820

My daughter Georgia was born on day   10,431
My son Jaedon was born on day   11,526
That's approximately 31.5 years (ish).

But how long do I have left? Well, I guess that if I live to 75 years of age (hopefully more) then I have approximately 16,660 days left to live! Now at first glance, that sounds like a lot, but let's take a few things into account:

16,660 days to live *BUT* ...
I lose 2,288 days because I have 1 day off a week
So I have 14,372 days left.
I lose 834 days because I take 20 minutes a day in the
    toilet, shaving etc.
So I have 13,690 days left.
I lose 591 days because I watch 1 hour of TV a day.
So I have 12,856 days left.
I lose 591 days because I drive 1 hour a day
So I have 12,265 days left.
I lose 1,440 days because I have 4 weeks holiday a year
So I have 11,674 days left.
I lose 591 days because I am on the phone 1 hour a day
So I have 10,234 days left.
And I lose other days for other random things like
    queuing in MacDonald's and other random places
    (and don't forget I have to sleep occasionally too!)

So, of the 16,660 days, according to my statistics, I only really have 10,234 days left. Now it's clearly not rocket science and I am sure there things I have missed etc., *but the point is this:* there's isn't a lot of time after all.

My days are numbered! Incidentally – yours are too!

Pulling out tooth #8

Once upon a time I dreamed of what it would be like to be 17. Now I am 32 and I realise, time is flying by. Soon my son and daughter will be sitting down on the grass, thinking about the car they will be driving (or flying)! Time is tickin' away! Choose to redeem the time, so it really works for you! How do you do that?

1. Remember your Creator!
2. Remember the comeback King is coming
3. Number your days

Next time the devil tries to tell you that you have lots of time, remember, he's lying! Tell him your days are numbered and then remind him that his days are too. He hates that stuff! In fact, read Revelation 22:21 to him. It says; *"The grace of the Lord Jesus be with God's people. Amen"*

What's that got to do with anything? Well, Genesis 1:1 says: *"In the beginning God ... "* and Revelation finishes with *"Jesus"*. No mention of the devil, *why?* Because his days were numbered, God was counting and his days ran out!

Coming up

THE END!

Making it real for you!

1. How do you think "Remembering your Creator" will help you as you live life on a daily basis?

   . . . .
   . . . .
   . . . .
   . . . .

2. If you knew that Jesus was coming back in seven days, what three things would you make sure you do this week?

   . . . .
   . . . .
   . . . .

3. On a separate piece of paper, why not "Number your days"?

4. Write a prayer, asking God's help so you can make the most of the time available to you to accomplish all that God has in store for you.

   . . . .
   . . . .
   . . . .
   . . . .

The last bit!

So there you go! If I was the devil, I would be working over time right now to reinforce everything you've just read in this book. I would,

- Tell you, "You are a victim *not* a victor."
- Tell you, "It is too late to change."
- Tell you, "That'll do – you've read the book, that's enough."
- Distract you from ever really embracing God and His purposes for your life.
- Help you find excuses as to why you can never change.
- Get you to compare yourself to someone else.
- Get you to take the easy option.
- Tell you, "You've got loads of time."

If I was you, I'd remind the devil that you are wise to his tricks and that living for Jesus is the most amazing thing in the world. And to make it worse, I'd probably read the book again and make sure I really do the "Making it real for you" pages. After that I'd get up, get out and make a difference for God in the world.

> *Question* – Why did the chicken cross the road?
> *Answer* – Because it could!

Question – How can you live a champion life?
Answer – Because with God, you can!

I believe in you! You are awesome!!!

Coming up...

If I had a face like yours!

Contact details

All enquiries regarding this publication and Glyn Barrett's speaking engagements should be made to:

V3 Leadership
The Megacentre
Sheffield
S2 5BQ
United Kingdom

Tel: +44 (0)114 272 5077
Email: info@v3leadership.com

Information and resources can be found at:

www.v3leadership.com
www.hopecity.co.uk
www.youth-alive.co.uk